opponent's body. When this energy goes t
provokes internal damage.

This is particularly evident in palm blows. Pain is felt inside, often far from the point of impact.

The body produces a short-width wavy movement, especially in the backbone, which makes possible to launch powerful blows in short distance with little run.

Most of styles using this principle apply it in round techniques (Tai Chi, for example) or shoves. One of the features of WT is the development of this principle into fist and palm straight blows as well as uppercuts, etc.

However, getting the required coordination to organize movements (micro-movements, in fact) of the various parts of the body into a single technique is not as easy as it looks.

For instance, if you start the leg movement first and then the arm follows, the technique will fail; it will be a blow given merely by the arm. If your arm is the first to move, then the body will work better, provided there is no delay. The ideal, as usual, is unity, but one rule must be observed: the body goes behind the blow to provide support to it.

The training method should consist of starting the blow and immediately creating the wavy body movement described above.

The time between this two stages will be progressively reduced until the gap is virtually nil. And why not the other way round?

Condition 3: Use your bodyweight by moving

Try this test: launch a blow with a forward step:

A. Move your body first, then the fist.

B. Launch your fist and use the inertia for the step.

Method "A" consists in moving the body first and then the fist. It implies three disadvantages:

1. It is slower.
2. It is less powerful.
3. You are unprotected.

This is a method widely used in gyms, so it is worth to analyze it. It is slower because it is easier to start moving a small inert mass than a bigger one.

1. Moving our fist first is faster than moving our whole body, as we are creating inertia which can be drawn upon to start the step faster and effortlessly.

2. The blow will be less powerful, as it will not be supported by the body mass, which arrived first.

3. This is the most dangerous point, head and trunk advancing first are exposed to our opponent's hits.

Conclusion: Simultaneousness is an ideal, a reference, perfection. To achieve it, if this can be achieved, the right way is to start the blow first and let it draw the body behind it; never the other way round.

Condition 4: Get your gravity center down

This principle can be applied in two ways:

A. Taking advantage of ground reaction.

B. Taking advantage of "falling".

Method "A" has been described already. When the gravity center goes down, our feet press the ground, thus generating a reaction force which will be transmitted trough the body wavy movement to our arm or leg, as described above.

Example: the straight blow of Siu Nim Tao form.

Method "B" is more common. We let out bodyweight to fall down to support our blow. This is so evident in hooks, in side blows such as Fak Sao, in downward elbows, etc.

Condition 5: Use your opponent's strength against him and add yours

The most evident example of this principle is the el Passive Moving Turn. To understand it, imagine a revolving doll, arms outstretched. If we suddenly push one of its arms, the doll will go round and hit us with the other arm, giving us back our own force. This is a passive turn.

WT's Passive Moving Turn is similar, but there are two differences which provide greater efficiency:

1. We do not rotate on the axis. The axis moves off the attack-line, using our opponent's strength in the same way (translation).

2. We add our force to his, giving him back his force "plus interest".

One side of our body will be Yin and give way, and the other side will be Yang and hit, thus achieving "sımultaneous attack and defense".

The spring-body

All these data enable us to start understanding what "soft styles" are about. Applying these principles will produce a style with relatively long movements, plenty of displacements with changing positions and marked variations of the gravity center. This can be observed in styles such as Tai Chi, Aikido, etc. For instance, when shoved, you would give way stepping backwards and turning, or bending down to a very low position.

In WT a very subtle work exists which some people compared to the ABS braking system in cars, enabling you to absorb great forces with so little movement of your own body.

The effect is "eating" your opponent's force while giving way at the same time. Te body, just like a spring, "compresses" against the ground, accumulating force taken from the attack in the form of "potential energy". It then "explodes" in the form of kinetics, hitting through the gap created when neutralizing the attack, according to the principle of reaction, produced from bringing the gravity center down as explained above.

This is the action mechanism of sticky-legs techniques, through which low kicks, sweep kicks, etc. can be canceled out. In hand techniques, Fook Sau, Tan Sau, Wu Sau and Bong Sau are evident ways of applying this principle.

By developing this "human spring", a great economy of movement and "mountain-like" stability in stance are achieved, as all the force provided by your opponent is directed (using the body in the reverse way of the blow-launching chain) through your arm, scapulae, backbone, pelvis, hip, knees and feet against the ground, hammering you in. The bigger the pressure, the more firm your support on the ground (and the greater the force of the hit when you "release the spring"). Additionally, we can keep on going forward to the enemy while absorbing his force.

So, how can this be learned? Theory and practice are very different.

CHAPTER II
The training method

WT uses a technical scheme to achieve the "flowing body

1. Free from your own force

The first thing we have to learn is to control our own muscles to keep them free from unnecessary tensions. In WT we practice SNT form (see Siu Nim Tao chapter) to train relaxing our trunk and arms while strongly working our legs in the adduction position. Muscular control, placing joints in the correct angles and using elbows as drivers for all movements are exercised here.

Other valuable method is the wall punch-bag, where the straight-punch burst, the kicks, etc. are practiced. The aim is not to get harder fists and feet, but to achieve movement relaxation, as well as speed, power and fluidity.

It is relatively easy to stay relaxed when performing movements into the air, but things get harder when movements have to be applied to an opponent. This is the reason why training with a partner must be practiced.

2. The 4 basic reactions

If we consider the human body by sectors —upper extremities, lower extremities, trunk and

10

head— exercises can be developed to apply each of the 4 basic reactions to each part.

Our opponent can apply his force in four main directions, and we can take advantage of it by using the four basic reactions.

To understand these reactions, we would explain how do they work in the case of the arm. You can draw various exercises for the trunk, head and lower body from this example.

Our right arm is half-flexed in front of us, hand at breastbone level, in the central line of our body. Attacks directed to our central line can contact two zones – the inner zone, which we will call (i), inside the arm; and the outer zone, called (o). Our opponent can press our inner zone in two ways:

1. **Outwards.**
2. **Inwards.**

In the first case, the basic reaction is to raise the elbow and let the force go to the outer zone. This reaction is called "Kao Sau", **(Ppcture 11)**

In the second case, the basic reaction is to go with it and, when a gap is created, to hit going forward. This reaction is called "Pak Sao" if the contact is at the hand level. If contact is made in the forearm, it is called "Jam Sao" (see Cham Sao **picture 12).**

Our opponent can press our outer zone in two ways:
1. **Crossing the line.**
2. **Not crossing the line.**

In the first case, we raise our elbow and follow our opponent's movement. This technique is called "Bong Sau", **(picture 13).**

In the second case we put our elbow in and turn the palm upwards, giving way to his arm and using the gap so created to hit our opponent. This technique is called "Tan Sao", **(picture 14).**

There are two more alternatives: our opponent can use his right or left arm. Tan Sao is mainly applied when the attacker uses his left

hand, so we stay inside. If he attacks using his right hand, Tan Sao, Lop Sau (hold) or Yut Sau can be suitable.

These are the four basic reactions. Vertical components (top-down or bottom-up pressure) and highness level (high, low or middle) conform the resulting full array of possibilities.

3. Passive Moving Turn

What happens when our opponent attacks while moving forward through our central line? In this case, we have to apply the Passive Moving Turn, using his strength to get off the attack-line and giving it back to him. This way, the four reactions and the passive turn are combined.

Training method-forms

1. Darn Chi Sao (one hand stuck). This exercise is used to learn:
• The four basic reactions.
• The passive turn.
• Feeling the gap.
• Moving forward with a step, keeping contact.

2. Application: Lat Sao. Role-playing to put into practice the acquired sensitivity (see chapter).

3. Chi Sao with both hands: Rolling (Poon Sao). Now both hands are contacting simultaneously. Used to learn how to react with each hand independently, applying the four basic reactions, as well as to relax and keep forward pressure at the same time. No steps are practiced.

4. Chi Sao sections. Created by Great Master Leung Ting. From the previously explained base, the student starts practicing the first Chi Sao section. He/she will perform the necessary movements to develop the following qualities while staying relaxed
• Hitting with the whole body.
• Using the gravity-center fall.
• Coordinating punch and step.
• Developing the "human spring".
• Passive turn.
• "Breaking" the guard and get in.

Displacements are continuous, thus greatly improving passive turns. Sections match up with the various levels and forms. For instance, in the first technician grade, four different sections are learned, with an increasingly difficulty level. Each section is based on the previous one and it develops our qualities with harder exercises. They are then applied to Lat Sao. With each section, our "tensions" and hindrances to improve our "adaptability" are gradually filed off.

The sections scheme comprise all levels up to the fifth technician grade. Each form integrates the appropriate sections to develop all principles when training with a partner.

5. Chi Gerk: "sticky legs", which are worked in the sections referred above.

Complementary exercises:
• Wall punch-bag. Aimed to develop "relaxed force" and speed in punches and kicks. It also corrects errors in straight-punch direction

(if direction is wrong, your hand will rub the bag and your skin can get scratched). If we feel our blows "powerful", the contrary will be probably the case. If we have a great feeling of "force" when working on punches, it is definitely a sign that we are involving more "muscle breaks", less relaxation and less real power. Thus the punch-bag is a very important item.
- Steps (with a wide variety of possibilities).
- Power exercises (carried out in pairs).
- Arm-techniques.
- Leg-techniques.

The two latter groups of exercises are aimed to improve the way of using knees and elbows and to strengthen agonist muscles used in the techniques.
- Physical conditioning (optional): suppleness, strength, etc. WT requires less suppleness than other martial styles, and you don't need to be a muscle-head to practice it. However, the student may wish to improve those qualities, which are definitely beneficial. To achieve this goal, we recommend isometric and eccentric contraction stretching and lifting weights imitating WT movements.

6. The wooden dummy

Wooden-dummy training is not aimed to harden, as many people think. The wooden dummy form is used to train the most advanced footwork of WT, which enables us to reach the back of our opponent while hitting him with both arms and one leg.

We also learn to absorb shocks against an invincible rigid force (the wooden dummy stays immovable).

In any case, a living creature is much better than the "Chong". This device is useful when a training partner is not available.

7. The long stick

The long stick training is aimed to apply the principles explained above through a rigid inanimate object.

The added difficulty is the stick's rigidness. When we get a blow from other stick, we must flex like a spring and keep contact to take advantage of the gap which will be created and to control the enemy's stick movements. Just to get an idea of what this means, hold a stick, at least 2.5 meters long, with both hands in the last forty centimeters of it. Make someone else to hit the other side of your stick with another pole, applying maximum power and speed. Your stick will be violently pulled apart by the force exerted.

The Chi Kwan (sticky stick) training tries to avoid this. When taking the other stick's blow, ours must give way to it, thus eliminating the shock, while keeping stuck to it conforming a single unit. In that moment, the opponent is lost. He cannot attack and, if he tries to snatch our weapon away, he will create a gap which we could use to attack.

Due to the stick's length, driving errors are magnified. A small mistake of your hand is converted into a great deviation in the other side of the stick.

Additionally, this weapon's weight is another added difficulty element. In this case, full body coordination is taken to a higher level.

An ever-refining process

The beginner is a knot of tensions and resistances of which he is not even aware. Attaining a psycho-physical condition of fluidity in every situation is not a one-step process; it does not take a couple of years neither. This is quite frustrating because, when you think you have achieved something, your Sifu will expose you to a more advanced exercise and all tensions and errors will then reappear. Thus, every time a layer of tensions, unnecessary resistance or even "ignorance" in certain sense (as we said, intelligence = adaptability) is removed, another deeper layer which we were not aware of arises. When our arms appear to be "flowing", we discover that shoulders, backbone or hips are indeed acting as inanimate blocks we don't know how to move. When executing the forms we are so relaxed but... hey, when someone shove us, hit our hands or whatever, the body –and mind!– becomes an immovable hard piece for a moment, prey of panic and surprise. No adaptation! No Tao law!

Training with our Sihings or Sifus shows us up. We do not notice their strength, they are apparently void, no pressure. But when we try to get into the pretended gap we get a blow. Surprise! There was pressure, however minimum. Their pressure is so low that we cannot even notice it, while ours is so scandalously obvious for them.

This is one of the main keys; our ability is progressively refined. The greater the difference between pressures, the easier to take advantage of the force. That is the reason why when we get in contact with an expert we do not feel anything. It looks fluffy, asleep. He, on the contrary, perceives our body better than ourselves. Sometimes it seems that he is reading our mind. There is an explanation for this apparent mystery. Our intentions create unconscious movements, even before the idea becomes conscious. That is what he perceives through contact.

For some people, this can be magic. For the skilled person, is just routine. Thus, the development never ends.

A new body

The expression of all concepts referred above into a movement during a combat requires to develop some qualities which are not usual at all. It implies using the neuromuscular system in a specialized way. For instance, getting to keep forward pressure and to give way at the same time. These two actions are totally different. Our brain is not naturally programmed to perform these actions simultaneously. It is necessary to accomplish new learning on moving and coordinating muscle groups according to a series of patterns unknown to our species.

Additionally, unintelligent reflex responses must be removed. This is the case of the sinewy reflex provoked by a muscle being contracted, or its backward movement when under attack. All this requires training, attention, reflection and continuous correction. WT offers a really new principle. The average person, when confronted to a force, only recognizes two possible reactions:
- To resist, shoving to counteract this force hoping to overcome.
- To give way, letting himself be crushed, resigning, getting carried away. Being destroyed, in a word.

None of this reactions is successful. WT offers an intermediate way. By intermediate we mean different, beyond both extremes; not sometimes letting be crushed and sometimes resisting. On the contrary, the WT fighter never lets himself be crushed and never resist. He acts upon a different principle. He always win by adapting himself with advantage.

Applications to different fields
1. In sports

Some high-competition sportspeople can improve their results by learning methods such as Chi Sao and taking regular WT training:

Judokas, Olympic wrestlers and Thai Boxers could probably be the most benefited from these techniques.

In this sense, coaches from the Bulgarian national wrestling team introduced Chi Sao in their athletes training. The Bulgarian team is composed by Olympic and world champions, and they decided to adopt this method after seeing how their best wrestler was unable to catch Sifu K. R. Kernspecht even once, although strict rules had been previously agreed upon: prohibition of all kind of blows and exclusive use of hand-to-hand techniques. So, even without 80% of his arsenal, Sifu Kernspecht was able to neutralize and cut every attack from the (Olympic and world champion) wrestler, just by flowing and giving way. This match is video-recorded. Since then, Bulgarian coaches study Chi Sao to improve their results.

2. In self-defense

Obviously, taking advantage of our opponent's force and being able of hitting with our whole body are excellent qualities to defend ourselves against an aggression.

3. In disability rehabilitation

These exercises can be used to rehabilitate neuromuscular problems in a more entertaining and rich way than traditional physiotherapy.

4. In free fight combats (UFC, Vale-Tudo)

Many people wonder how can they neutralize grapplers' techniques.

In 1997, in the July issue of Black Belt Magazine (Spanish Edition) we explained the training method. With the ideas contained in the present lines we can understand the core, what makes it work.

To take someone to the ground, he must oppose some resistance, i.e. exert any kind of force. Of course, his force must be less than ours, that is the reason why take-downs always use levering systems.

For instance, you rush at your opponent's leg, passing under his attack, hold his legs with your arms (fixed point) and shove his belly with your shoulder. Another option - if his weight is on his front leg, you sweep it or hold or block it and then use your arms to hold his arms (or head or shoulders) and you use a pair of forces to hurl him.

Once on the floor, this process goes on - to apply a lock, a supporting point is required. Without a support, we cannot gear. That easy.

But we must not fool ourselves. Theory is easy, now try to take it down to practice. Ask a 170-pound guy with some kind of grappling experience to try to take you down. He will probably crush you. An adequate training method is required to achieve this goal. We need to start slowly in order to feel his strength and to not instinctively tense our body but intelligently giving way and hitting at the same time. The difficulty should then gradually increase, thus refining our "adaptability". This should be tried in various situations, angles, standing up, on the floor, kneeling, etc. Let your training partner "catch" you a little bit more each time and practice your escape.

The most important thing here is PATIENCE. The different WT programs cover all these requirements. If we train with a qualified instructor, we can get it.

Our next step would be mental application of the "non-resistance" principle, the base of Buddhist and Taoist meditation.

CHAPTER III
The Yin-Yang harmony in the psychological field: The Art of Meditation

Buddhism has been defined as the intermediate path; beyond indulgence and repression, it does not give into pleasure and does not constrain itself. Just like WT at a physical level, Buddhism does not let itself to be carried away and neither resist at a psychological level. Three philosophies are studied in WT:

• **Taoism:** applied in strategy and physical implementation of techniques, as well as in medicine, healthcare and energy.
• **Buddhism:** to learn freedom and mental stability. It is the art of meditation and maintaining a powerful mind through a positive attitude.
• **Confucianism:** to govern family relationships: master-student, veteran-new students, pedagogy and ethics.

This chapter provides a description of the art of Buddhist meditation and its close connection with WT Chi Sao.

Analogy of chi sao and meditation

Chapter I explains how to apply the principle of Yin and Yang to WT. Follows and explanation of how to apply this principle to the meditation field.

The Yin aspect refers to relaxation, non-reaction to any phenomenon. Whether the feeling is pleasant or unpleasant, the mind stays relaxed, passive, no reaction.

Some examples: you are meditating and you start feeling itchy. The immediate reaction of any one is to identify this itching as an unpleasant sensation and scratch. If it does not work, you will probably get anxious and think how irritating it is and how much you would like to get rid of it. Maybe you will get a cream but, if the itching persist, your distress will grow and you could even fall into a depression.

This reaction is analogous to Chi Sao, where the person tries to resist his opponent's strength using an opposite force. In this case, we are dealing with physical forces, and in the previous example it was mental forces, but actually the underlying principle is the same: resistance, rejection.

Now, what would be the meditator's reaction in this situation? Expert meditator will not react to the stinging feeling. He will not assess it as good or bad. He will not even identify it as "itchy". He will stay out of any kind of conception or reaction about what it is going on.

It goes beyond the idea of a meditator meditating about something, or an "I" who feels or perceives anything. When removing those concepts, suffering ceases to exist. There is no "I" who feels itching, not even the concepts of "me" or "itch". There is no duality, thus there is no suffering. This is analogous to Chi Sao: you give way to your opponent's strength while keeping stuck to him. In both instances we find fluidity, harmony, no friction.

What happens if the feeling is pleasant? The common sensations of sexual pleasure could be used as an example (during meditation, sensations more pleasant than sexual can be felt, but this example is preferable as it is known by everyone). The average man or woman will react with attachment. He or she will identify the feeling as pleasant, and immediately reactions and conceptions will appear — fear to lose this feeling, fear that it does not last, fear to be unable to repeat it, wish to repeat it, and in this case, wish to intensify it, as repeating reduces sensitivity. If this feeling cannot be achieved, anger or depression will follow.

What would be the meditator's reaction? The meditator will not assess the feeling and will not think about it. It will live it as is, without anticipating its end or thinking about future. It will enjoy without attachment, fearless then. Once it is extinguished, he will forget it; he will not think about it again. If the feeling repeats, great, if it does not, great. This is an analogous concept to the WT principle of "do not let yourself be crushed or carried away by your opponent's force". Giving way and letting being crushed is similar to being attached to pleasant feelings in meditation. WT does not resist, and does not draws or crush. Likewise, the meditator does not reject or resist unpleasant feelings and neither sticks to or pursues pleasant feelings. He is levelheaded.

The application of the giving-way principle has been explained in the mental field, the Yin aspect. But, what about Yang? It is lucidity, penetrating intelligence which can understand the real nature of phenomena.

When the meditator perceives something, he understands its nature at the moment –intuitively, directly–. He understands that any phenomenon is temporary, so it is nonsense sticking to or resisting it.

He knows that no phenomenon has an "I" with own existence; there is no meditator, meditation or object. In Buddhist meditation, the Yin passive aspect of calm and relaxation is called SAMATHA in Sanskrit (CHIH in Chinese). The Yang or intelligence aspect is called VIPASYANA in Sanskrit (Kuan in Chinese). Perfect meditation is the combination of both, which leads us to the awakening.

In Chi Sao, the principle of forward pressure represents the Yang aspect – it is analogous to lucidity or penetrating intelligence in meditation. When practicing Chi Sao, a loss of pressure means a loss of conscience, a loss of lucidity in fact.

For a moment, a loss of conscience is an opening, a gap, a loss of intelligence, freedom; in meditation is a distraction.

The Yin aspect (SAMATHA, CHIH) of meditation is trained by concentrating on an object and resting on it. For instance, paying attention to the body feelings, to breathing, avoiding any reaction, without falling asleep or distracting.

The Yang (VIPASYANA, Kuan) aspect of meditation is learned by questioning ordinary concepts. For instance, you wonder "¿who is meditating"? If your mind replies "I do", ask again! "Where is "I"?, etc. This is the origin of Koan (Kung An in Chinese) of Zen Buddhism (Chan en chino). I hope this brief description is useful to outline the way in which WT physically expresses the same principle meditation expresses mentally; adaptability and no duality.

Sifu Víctor Gutiérrez 35

36 The Tao of the action

2nd PART
How to practice WT Chi Sao

CHAPTER I
Concepts and strategy

What do concepts and strategy really mean and how can they be conveyed to martial arts and training?

Almost everybody has heard about concepts or strategy but, do we really know what are them about, or they are just words we have heard from a Master some time?

In our training, we frequently find that, although our style -whatever it is- should be influenced by some kind of strategy, we get lost in meaningless details which eventually block our perspective. We must understand that philosophy, concept or strategy are the foundations of our style. We should ask ourselves if we really understand their meaning and get identified with it. Rather than finding an idol or famous fighter that makes us confident that our style is the most appropriate for us, we should discover what is the driving force which inspired us to practice martial arts and consequently find the art which matches our projections. Next step would be trying to understand its strategy or concepts, as this would be the basis of all that will be done. When performing a movement or exercise, I must wonder if what I am doing is a true reflection of the concepts or just a copy of a movement taught by my instructor which I perform like a Xerox machine. Up to now, martial arts have been surrounded by a mystic aura conferring the instructor or Master the "right" to avoid explanations. Do not allow yourself to be deceived by these excuses. Insist to get a concrete explanation the objective of the exercise you are performing and the general concept it is due to. Every martial art is exposed to a strategy, and movements and exercises performed should be due to this strategy. Which one is the best for you depends on many factors, such as strength, speed, explosiveness, weight, age, etc. It is necessary to bear all these in mind to find the most suitable style for you. Other factors should be considered, such as what do you expect from the chosen style: just to be fit?, winning tournaments?, you like competition?, you want to be able to defend yourself and feel more confident? Once this is decided, you should analyze the styles which are interesting for you and try if you have the physical and mental conditions required to develop their strategy. If you get carried away by a sudden passion, you are lost.

Setting aside the way in which you should choose your style, now we would give an overview of most existing martial arts' strategies. We could establish four general groups.

1. Blocking-counterattack: the aim is to visually locate the attack, block it and counterattack . A great deal of explosiveness and vision is required; the training should be oriented to develop the skills required to successfully develop this strategy. Fighting concepts:

- Keeping distance.
- Visual perception of the attack.
- Speed, strength, explosiveness.
- Ability to react quickly.

2. Protective shield: our arms or legs will be used as a shield in front of us, moving constantly in order to provide no static target to our enemy. Any gap in his defense will be used to attack. Great explosiveness is also required, as well as vision and physical condition. The strategy will be:

- Mobility.
- Visualization of defense gaps.
- Optical trick.
- Speed, explosiveness, power.
- Keeping distance.

3. Wrestling: the idea is to close up distance between you and your enemy to avoid his blows. Once reached, you try to immobilize or throttle him. It is necessary to learn how to break-up distance and use the physical exhaustion of your enemy to throttle him o dislocate any joint. High level of stamina is required to exhaust your opponent. The strategy consist on:

- Closing-up distance.
- Take the enemy to the floor.
- Physical exhaustion of the opponent.
- Stamina.
- Strength.
- Strain detection.

4. Adaptable: There is no specific purpose but protecting the own body deploying natural weapons towards the enemy to detect his plans and act accordingly. the main concepts in these styles are:

- Going towards the enemy.
- Contacting him.
- Taking advantage of his strength.
- Using the sense of touch to detect his plans.
- Adaptation.

As aforesaid, most styles have many factors in common. There are differences, however meaningless. Their principles and strategic foundations are very similar. Actually, the first two strategies or concepts are so similar that, in fact, are the same. So, martial styles can be reduced to three main groups:

A. Those trying to keep distance.
B. Those trying to close up distance.
C. Those trying to adapt to the opponent.

The first strategy is aimed to maintain the enemy out of reach, but in fact this is virtually impossible --if I want to hit him, I have to enter in reach, thus contradicting my own strategy.

The second is its true opposite. This is more realistic, as no confrontation exists without physical contact. It offers the chance to close up distance and try to bring him to floor, to your field.

The third one is the most convincing for a number of reasons. In the previous strategies an important fact is missing: each person is different and can act the way he/she wants. So, those strategies can fail under a number of circumstances, as they are based on (i) strength, speed, explosiveness and physical condition, and (ii) on the assumption that you are able to keep the enemy on a distance or close it up. From my point of view, it is not sensible to base one's style on assumptions. It is necessary to know what is really in danger and trying to use our natural weapons in a way which protects our weak points at all times, also adapting to every attempt of the enemy. To achieve that, the focus should not be the movements I have to perform to successfully protect my personal safety. There is an invariable fact: if your opponent wants to harm you, he must get close to your body to perform his/her chosen action. The battlefield is my body, so if I manage to use my arms and legs as "antennas" pointed at the enemy, he/she will be forced to push them aside to get to me. It is then when my tactile sensitivity goes into action: their movements and strength are used in my advantage, without the need of studying any kind of potential attack to successfully defend myself.

This is the great myth of martial arts: to use the enemy's strength in my advantage, and improve and evolve through the years. Evolution and improving ability even late in life cannot be based on strength nor an assumption. Our opponent's intention are never known. The only truths are the place where our body is found, the fact that my enemy must get closer to reach me, and the impossibility, as years go by, of basing a style on strength, speed, explosiveness physical condition and much less on an assumption. What is an "assumption"? An assumption means the conviction that you are able to see, guess or know any kind of attack from your enemy; to believe you will manage to keep distance or to close it up. A good style must base the training objectives on the following:

1. To learn to assess distance.
2. To know our body's moving ability.
3. To increase adaptation ability through relaxation.
4. Psychological training.
5. The ability to keep vital space (to know vital space dimensions).
6. To increase body coordination.
7. To understand that these concepts are valid under every situation.
8. To believe in creativity (we are not all the same).

Never learn by heart the exercises you perform in training. Your objective must be to increase your physical and mental skills. Your training must be oriented to go beyond the mere knowledge of certain movements. Ask your instructor the objective of every exercise to get a better understanding of your art's concepts and the influence of every exercise on the improvement of any aspect of those concepts. This is the only way of going beyond the mere performance of a movement and, with time, you will assimilate the concepts and thus convert the art you practice into an attribute of your own, a way to express your own personality.

Remark
• Understand the concepts and strategy of your style; look for them in every exercise you practice and do not get lost in technical details.
• Always keep your concepts clear in mind and check if they work in any situation.

詠 春 拳

44 The Tao of the action

CHAPTER II
One technique vs. one million

What does usually determine that a martial artist have a more advanced level than another? Why do we say that one system is more comprehensive than other?

The most probable answer would be: "MASTERING A GREATER AMOUNT OF TECHNIQUES". In a combat, we cannot anticipate the movements of our enemy, so the more techniques we have trained to perfection, the more the resources we will have. This idea underlies the belief that the more years of practice the higher the level reached; a greater diversity of offensive and defensive movements would have been learned and trained. Following this reasoning to the comparative study of different styles, it is natural to say that a method integrating one hundred techniques is superior to another comprising only fifty techniques. In fact, in any field of knowledge or life we observe this rule: an engineer, a doctor or a lawyer are more effective in their jobs if they acquire more knowledge and expertise. Thus, when we say that a person has more experience than another, we are stating that he/she has a better knowledge because he/she has seen and lived more. In short, he/she relies on more information. However, in real fight, a self-defense situation, there is a crucial difference in relation to other activities or jobs. I refer to real fight, not sport. In sport, the enemy can be studied months in advance, and specific trainings can be set up according to his/her characteristics (right/left-handed, preference for long/short distance, favorite techniques, etc.). Boxers, Vale-Tudo and UFC fighters or soccer players act this way. Also, during the sports event, breaks and stops provide time to think and be instructed by the coach.

In real fight, nothing is predictable, everything is unknown: enemy, date, time, place... even what will I be doing. And most important - THERE IS NO TIME to think. A doctor or lawyer at work have time to think, analyze or even consult what they can do. A fighter does NOT. Probably real fight is the only human situation in which we need an INTELLIGENT response to a life-or-death problem without thinking or reasoning our reaction.

Because of this, the most frequent motto is that techniques must be trained until they become automatic and unconscious. Maximum speed will then be achieved and defense will be as effective as possible.

Do you agree with the arguments expressed heretofore? If you do, I have bad news for you. IT IS PHYSIOLOGICALLY IMPOSSIBLE to be as quick as the attacker. Wait, take your time to think about this and let me explain some facts:

First, a description of the defense process against any attack:

1. Detect attack.
2. Recognize its characteristics (path, objective, etc.).
3. Elect response (technique to employ).
4. Perform technique.

And no time to think. Of course, we are talking about experts, not beginners.

Now, we need to establish what is the minimum time required by the nervous system to carry out the process above. To this end, an experiment can be made; starting in the most favorable conditions possible:

- Psychologically: no fear, insecurity or surprise element.
- Prepared and ready, in the best body position.
- Knowing in advance the attack to be launched and its target (straight punch to the chest, right hand). No need to recognize the attack or choose a response.
- Knowing the moment of the attack, counting 1-2-3.
- No deceiving movements or feints by the opponent. Just the punch.
- Defender should be a recognized expert in his style -national team or similar-.

Even in this undisputedly favorable conditions, no expert has been able to systematically defend a straight punch from medium distance without preparation. Most people missed all the ten possible hits. The few best of them managed to block one of the ten blows. What would happen in a real situation, being attacked unexpectedly, ignoring the type of blow and target and feints in the menu?

The cause of this inability is that, no matter the fighting quality of the fighter, brain takes a second-tenth to activate and "plug-in" to react. We have a second-tenth delay to start with.

However, the brain still have to process the data, to assimilate what is coming, and that is the next step. For most blocking/dodging styles, this means to establish:

- The height to which the attack is heading for: up (face), medium (trunk), low (genitals or legs).
- If it comes right or left = SIDE.
- In many cases, the form of the attack (straight, round).
- Other elements such as speed, obliqueness, center/side direction, etc. which are not considered here.

In practice, for a right-hook punch to the face, using a counterattack of dodging and punch to the liver, the process would be as follows:

As it is showed in the chart, before being able to defend ourselves,

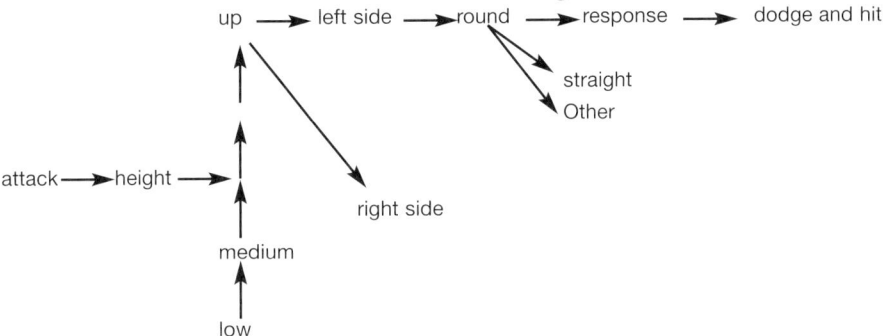

we would have to complete several choice processes (unconscious, as explained above) to recognize the attack. Then, we would have to complete a second process to decide which technique from our arsenal to use and perform it.

There are three elements: 3 height levels x 2 sides x 2 paths = 12 elements (actually, many more).

Brain takes 0.745 seconds (including activation time) to choose 1 of these 12 elements.

A really quick expert would need 0.15 seconds to perform a movement, which means 6.6 blockings per second (a very optimistic estimation). Adding these two numbers, (0.746 + 0.150) the result is 0.896 seconds; the minimum time required to systematically block (that is 100% of attacks) any attack.

Actually, a real expert does not need such a long time. The reason is not that he/she "breaks" any natural law, but that he/she does not wait to ACCURATELY recognize the attack. On the basis of his/her experience, he/she FORESEES the attack before it is performed. This is due to the so-called PRE-PERCEPTION, which is quite easy to explain: virtually all of us perform almost imperceptible movements before the attack, slight tics in the eyes, elbows, knees, etc. An advanced fighter WOULD UNCONSCIOUSLY DETECT these tics and react ahead the attack, without having full certainty or security. This method entails two risks:

1. It does not guarantee systematic certainty (100%) as the attack is unknown.

2. We can be fooled by false preparation movements such as feints. Even so, 0.25 seconds (0.10 activation time + 0.15 = 0.25) are required to respond. A really quick expert would need 0.1-0.2 seconds in developing an attack movement. Draw your own conclusions.

At this point, it is obvious why traditional blockings are not often seen in tournaments: there is no time to perform them (except when the opponent is a beginner). Covering movements are used. Such movements are especially effective with 12 Oz. gloves. Bare-knuckle, hands cannot duly cover the head, so in self-defense are not valid.

Finally, we can draw some conclusions to sum all this up:

1. The greater the amount of techniques we know, the slower the reaction, as the response selection process is extended and so the reaction time.

2. In relation to the previous point, a style with a few effective techniques is better than other method comprising a lot of them.

3. If we need to establish the height, side and path of the attack in order to apply a defense, our possibilities are reduced to zero.

4. Attack is the best defense.

5. The best defense should be the one which requires a few or, even better, NO choice between different techniques and does not require attack recognition as the same movement would be effective for all.

6. The best defense should not depend on PRE-PERCEPTION to avoid being deceived by feints.

DOES THIS EXIST? DO YOU KNOW ANY METHOD WHICH COMPLIES WITH THESE CONDITIONS? I do. We call it "UNIVERSAL SOLUTION". It is a simple attack-defense movement (notice this feature!) used to hit and simultaneously defend ourselves against whatever aggression (weapons excluded), **(pictures 15, 16, 17, 18, 19).**

Sifu Víctor Gutiérrez

Universal Solution

Regardless the attack (any kind of foot/hand blows, sweepings, knocking-downs or throws) the movement is the same. Thus, the need of recognizing the attack to choose a defensive movement is avoided, saving a lot of time. Similarly, it does not entail "guessing" according to the pre-perception mechanism for the same reason.

"UNIVERSAL SOLUTION" is an ATTACK movement in which one approaches his/her opponent launching both arms and one leg in a way that he/she protects her/his own body while continuously launching blows towards the enemy. All his/her energy is headed to the center of the enemy's body. It is not necessary to pay attention to the movements of the opponent's extremities, so being deceived by feints is almost impossible.

"UNIVERSAL SOLUTION" is performed without any previous readiness (no slight movements that can alert enemy), using maximum economy of movement and the shortest path to reach the opponent with the aim of PASSING THROUGH him. To achieve this when training, exercises aimed to remove all "tics" which can betray us are practiced.

"UNIVERSAL SOLUTION" "EXPLODES" regardless what does the enemy do in the moment he enters the critic distance (maximum distance from which a kick can be launched without a previous step and reach us). The drive comes from our pelvis and shoot us forwards like a missile. So, another training aspect, is to learn how to feel this distance and resolutely move forward, not being influenced by feints, threats or gestures by our opponent.

The "UNIVERSAL SOLUTION" movement does not require an above-average suppleness and its effectiveness depend more on the angles adopted than on strength.

Just as important as technical advantages are PSYCHOLOGICAL ADVANTAGES. Faced with a panic situation, the most important thing is that fear should be translated into smart protective responses, not the contrary. Usually, an aggressor considers himself superior to and having advantage over his victim; otherwise he would not attack. In short, aggressor feels safer. Meanwhile, victim suffers fear and insecurity in proportion to the aggressiveness of the opponent. Under these circumstances, going back to block or dodge (besides having uncertain effectiveness) only increases disproportion. Victim would feel more inferior, ant aggressor would be stimulated and reinforced. Alternatively, if "UNIVERSAL SOLUTION" is applied, adrenaline produced by fear on the victim results in an explosion of energy headed towards the aggressor, surprising him with an AVALANCHE of blows which suddenly revert the situation: aggressor becomes totally outplayed by the "illogical" reaction of his victim and is forced to defend himself. He feels fear, while victim abandons his passive role and understands that aggressor is not so "formidable" and starts recovering self-confidence.

A great deal of time and effort (both hard to find nowadays) is required to master a technique. Bearing this in mind: Is it better to train a thousand techniques to address a thousand possible scenarios or to master one technique to defeat one million?

CHAPTER III
How to learn

WT is a martial art seeking maximum economy of movement. So, it requires special methods to achieve hitting power and to be able to take advantage of the enemy's force. Bluntness in short movements cannot be achieved using the same biomechanical principles as long-boxing styles such as Karate or traditional boxing. WT fighter must learn to use his/her muscle-skeletal system following co-ordination patterns completely different from the common principles. That is the greatest pitfall! The student has not the slightest reference in his brain to develop what is being required from him. Actually, his conditions are worse than if he were a newborn child who knows nothing and all he has to do is learn. WT student, also, must forget and de-program his brain against all those instinctive movement schemes repeated thousands of times throughout his entire life. The way to achieve this, the pedagogic tool available, lies in Chi Sao exercises. Chi Sao training follows some general principles aimed to make the student -or his brain, actually- unconsciously assimilate techniques. These principles are:
1. **Form - feeling.**
2. **Trial and error - ongoing correction.**
3. **Increasing difficulty.**
4. **Analyze and reflect.**
5. **Adapting speed.**
6. **Mutual co-operation - no competition.**
7. **Free improvisation.**
8. **Patience.**

1. Form - feeling

First of all, it is necessary to learn the "form", that is, the stance, the right angles. WT develops triangular biomechanics. Force is transmitted along lines forming triangles connecting each other, "traveling" along the body. The student learns the positions most favorable for this force transmission, as well as to move following optimum geometrical structures. This is one of the forms' functions.

Secondly, feeling is learnt. Through WT exercises, the student starts realizing that, when stances and movements are correct, the results are associated to a series of internal (proprioceptive) sensations. Gradually, as the difficulty of exercises increases, the student will be able to get a greater degree of control of his neuromuscular system and to identify those sensations more and more actively and consciously. Once this feeling is mastered, that is to say, once he has learn to consciously direct his force and absorb the enemy's through the internal transmission mechanisms, he can forget about the form. The "principle" is thus assimilated, so the "structure" is no longer required. So, he his totally free, he is WT.

2. Trial and error - ongoing correction

This principle is used to bring the student into a totally new world, where our conventional perceptions are NOT useful, where we see NOTHING, where we need guidelines and a learning method.

Sifu is our guide: traditionally, Wing Tsun masters had very few students. Chan Wah Sun, GM Yip Man's Sifu, had twelve students, almost a record. Under these conditions, Sifu practiced with the student and corrected him frequently. By trial and error, the student's brain unconsciously learned: Sifu stated that a movement was incorrect until the student, after searching with his mind "inside his body " guessed and managed to do it right. We have to bear in mind that the eye cannot convey the right "feeling" when practicing Chi Sao. The own student cannot identify it until the Master tells him. It is similar to learning bicycling: you fall and fall and suddenly once you manage to roll a few yards. Gradually, you can make more yards, without falling. This means that the brain starts knowing and recalling what did it do to keep balance. Finally, the process is mastered and you do not fall anymore. It must be noted that the whole learning process has been "proprioceptive", unconscious. Eyes did not make any contribution. Chi Sao is similar to this. No "falls" will dictate if we do exercises right or wrong. We need someone to tell us. Traditionally, Sifu, on private classes, took care of this task. However, when Master Yip Man opened WT to general public for the first time ever, the number of students rocketed and this method lost effectiveness. On regular classes, it was impossible that each student could be given this level of personal attention anymore. Only those who had financial resources to pay the higher-rate private classes with Sifu developed quickly. The same way you cannot learn bicycling "looking" at others doing it -as keeping one's balance is, above all, a feeling-, WT cannot be learned by the eye either. Chi Sao must be trained personally with the teacher, crossing arms and legs to "feel".

GM Leung Ting, knowing this problem severely limited the spread of WT, created exercises systems called "Chi Sao sections". Trough this sections, feelings of absorption and emission of force, as well as all technical principles of WT, could be learned without a teacher being present. The only thing you needed was a partner approximately the same level as you and to understand the foundations and objectives of each exercise. The same exercise conveys the student the trial - error - correction mechanism. Very cleverly, each exercise is designed in such a way that, if the student tries to develop a movement with wrong co-ordination, he cannot complete the movement and his partner breaks his balance or easily goes through his defense. Chi Sao sections do not substitute Sifu, but he is no longer forced to permanently and closely monitor the student. Thus, training with Sifu once in two or three months is enough. However, this requires a great deal of perseverance and responsibility from the student. If the student does not take an interest in training and pay attention to correct himself and "search inside" the feelings, no matter how many years he practices, he will not progress. Is a matter of quality, not quantity.

3. Increasing difficulty

Chi Sao sections -the first is presented in this book- corresponding to the student levels, embrace all the basis up to 5th technician grade, gradually increasing the difficulty level.

What is the aim of this progression? To get a more refined and effective development of the student's skills.

Each section makes it possible to file down our limitations and muscle tension in combat. Distance will get gradually shorter so forcing the student to multiply his resources to absorb forces and transmit power in a shorter and shorter distance. The practical result of this is that effectiveness in longer distances will greatly improve, becoming a cinch, and the student will be comfortable in previously difficult situations.

4. Analyze and reflect

This is the main pitfall for most WT students. In order to improve, it is necessary to constantly investigate what is being done wrong and how to correct it. As explained above, the student has no idea of how to properly control his movements. He can externally imitate movements but he soon becomes conscious that, although similar to those performed by the teacher, they do not work, there is a lack of neuromuscular operation activation. For this reason, in his training with a partner, attention must be paid in two directions:

- Outside: feel the partner in order to apply the four reactions and absorb the force he sends.
- nside: become conscious of his own body in order to form the mechanisms channeling the opponent's pressure to the ground, while deploying the own energy towards him.

If the student wants to progress, he must also reflect, try and analyze until he finds the right feelings. This reflection is simultaneously combined with practicing exercises; it is not something apart, sitting on a chair.

5. ADAPTING SPEED

In relation to the previous point, speed must be varied. There are some possibilities:
- Extremely slow.

- Slow.
- Medium.
- Fast.
- Explosive.

Slow speeds are necessary to work the internal consciousness of proprioceptive mechanisms and analyze them. They let us "seek" the sensations in muscles, joints, the stance and the coordinated order to be followed by different body parts.

Medium speed helps to remain focused both in feeling our partner and ourselves "inside".

The purpose of fast speed is more unconscious. In this case, chances of self-feeling and self-analyzing are limited; reactions are spontaneous.

Explosive speed is the real speed to apply the techniques, and is indicative of our true level regarding the use of softness, rooting and non-resistance principles in combat.

In any case, the five speeds must be trained. Usually, more time is devoted to slow and medium speed in Chi Sao. In spite of this, fast speeds must not be forgotten, as they are the "bridge" to Lat Sao (combat exercises). Many WT stylists dispense with explosive speed in training. The result is they cannot do anything with a real opponent.

6. Mutual co-operation - no competition

Some people misunderstand Chi Sao training as they insist on wining his partner. Some only seek to train with technically inferior people in order to keep their ego swell. Others get annoyed when some partners point out any execution failures and, trying to avoid this, choose more submissive buddies.

If you, dear reader, followed the reasoning which is broken down through this chapter, especially those relating to "try-error-correction method", it goes without saying that these attitudes are totally wrong and are a serious pitfall in the way to WT mastering.

Our training partner is like a mirror: it reveals what we cannot perceive by ourselves. If, for instance, you turn your shoulders an inch, thus rendering the technique useless, you will not realize about it unless someone makes you know. And that "someone" is the person with whom you are crossing arms. But, how? If you turn your shoulders, pressure will be deviated from the center. Your partner could easily take advantage of your strength and get to you. Only rising one shoulder would be enough. In that way, he will lose his connection to the ground and he could easily lose his balance. If your partner simply makes things easy for you, no matter how many years you train, your mistakes will stay the same and you will never improve.

Relationship between training partners is symbiotic: we help each other, mutually correcting. The better my partner the better me.

The higher the level of my partner the better their remarks and the greater my progress. So, it is preferable to choose a partner whose level is above ours so correction is permanent. Otherwise, if your partner is in a lower level, your mistakes will not be noticed by him, you will always defeat him, so you will not be able to correct your errors.

This mutual dependence, mutual aid, relationship is one of the most positive aspects of WT. Values rarely found in modern society, fond of competition and rivalry, can be thus learned. In WT, we evidently and clearly learn that helping others we can help ourselves. There is no sacrifice or abuse. Proper humbleness does not mean to "sacrifice" for others, get loose or let them pass over your head, but the acknowledgement that vanity is a hindrance for progress. We want to learn, but pride refrains us to take advice and corrections. So, in our own benefit, we should leave ego aside. We teach all we know in order to help our partner to progress, as the better he is, the better we can be. This way, we also forget any intention of abuse or imposition.

7. Free improvisation

Chi Sao training should not be limited to practicing Poon Sao or the sections; it must embrace free exercises. Both partners try to train and learn about their mistakes with maximum speed and spontaneity, moving at will. This kind of exercise is very important, but many students and instructors indeed suffer from lack of free practice, thus breaking the own foundations of WT - spontaneous adaptability to any situation.

8. Patience

Theoretical understanding of WT principles and mechanisms and its physical application do not develop equally. A sharp student may clearly understand what to do, but he cannot do it, he does not know how to translate it into effective motive actions. This situation can get really frustrating and create impatience and anxiety. Even though the student makes a swift progression, he may not realize about it and eventually drops. I have seen talented students hampered by this.

Advice: to learn WT, focus on the present and strive to the maximum, not paying too much attention to the final outcome. It will be here before you thought.

Remember that stubborn or conceited people cannot go far in WT. Their attitude is their main hindrance.

詠 春 拳

60 The Tao of the action

CHAPTER IV
Chi Sao progression

1ˢᵗ step: Introductory exercises

In the initial phase of training, the student should be given rudiments on the four basic reactions before starting one-hand Chi Sao. This is the reason why on the first student levels, a series of simple exercises is usually developed.

Exercises 1

Student in adduction stance, guard to the front **(see picture 20)**, right hand ahead. Instructor or partner pushes from the outside to the inside on the student's advanced arm. His response is Bong Sao **(picture 21)**. Back to he initial positions.

Now, the instructor pushes tangentially in the outside and the student reacts with Tan Sao **(picture 22)**. Instructor pushes from inside to outside in the interior part of the student's arm; he gives way to the force with Kau Sao **(picture 23)**. Back to the initial positions. Again, instructor pushes the interior part of the student's arm, tangentially to the inside this time. His response is Cham Sau **(picture 24)**. Back to the initial positions.

This exercises should be done without a preset order. Sometimes on one side, sometimes on the other, not following any fixed pattern. So, the student cannot anticipate his reaction and is forced to feel the movement. The key to guarantee the improvisation factor is that the student closes his eyes. Errors in angles and directions must be corrected at all times.

20

Sifu Víctor Gutiérrez 63

Exercise 2

In this exercise a new element is introduced. Along with the four reactions, the student is going to apply the "free-hand means punch" principle. In other words, now he has to detect energy gaps in the enemy's pressure and hit immediately through the gap created. While he provokes a Bong Sao, instructor raises his arm to hit the student in the upper part. If the student's pressure is headed forwards but he does not give way at the same time, he should unconsciously react with a punch. The same exercise can be performed from Tan Sao, as well as the subsequent reaction: palm or edge blow. Chan Sao and Kau Sao.

Exercise 3

Now, instructor attacks using techniques better headed towards the student's centre, stepping forward so forcing them to combine the four reactions with turns.

2nd step: Dan Chi Sao

Through the introductory exercises, the student starts getting familiar with basic concepts of WT. Then, he can start practicing one-hand Chi Sao.

If we compare exercises performed up to this point with Dan Chi Sao, we see that the latter is more subtle and precise. Dan Chi Sao movements are short, just inches-long in fact. If this margin is exceeded is because any of the following probably happened:
- The attack has not been absorbed by the relevant diluting reaction, so it "crosses the bridge" and reach its target (hits the chest).
- The attack is absorbed, because the defender gave way correctly. In this case, the attacker, after insisting, leaves a gap through which defender can hit, **(picture 25).**

With things as they are, if arms are fully stretched during one-hand Chi Sao, one can infer that execution is wrong and that the aim of the exercise has been misunderstood.

The attacker, on his part, should "listen" (to be alert for) the defender's reaction to know whether the way is clear -and he can hit- or the defense has been correctly performed thus creating an unrealized gap. In this latter case, the attacker must stick, defend himself, and

25

26

keep pressure forwards, "listening" at the same time, all of which happens in hardly thousandths of a second.

Progressing in Dan Chi Sao
1. Joining up the two springs

Subject A is in Fuk Sao and subject B in Tan Sao. Keeping this positions, it is possible to check if forwards pressure is correct and elastic. One pushes a little bit harder while the other gives way to him while keeping stuck and maintaining a certain degree of forwards pressure. Any energy gap is detected and taken advance of to hit. It is just like a spring; when you stop pushing it, it comes off, **(picture 27).**

2. Learning the movements

Once coupled, movements must be learned before performing free exercises.

• Group 1:

Fook-Tan position (see picture 27).
Palm-Chi Sao (see picture 28).
   Bong Sao - straight punch (see picture 29).
   Back to the start position (see picture 30).

- ## Group 2

    Subject "A", from FOOK, launches a blow tangentially.
    Subject "B" gives him way with a Tan Sao, **(picture 31, 32).**

• Group 3

Hand swap

System 1: Fook presses downwards; Tan Sao gives way to it and places above forming a Fook Sao. Then, the attacker must do a Tan Sao **(pictures 33, 34, 35).**

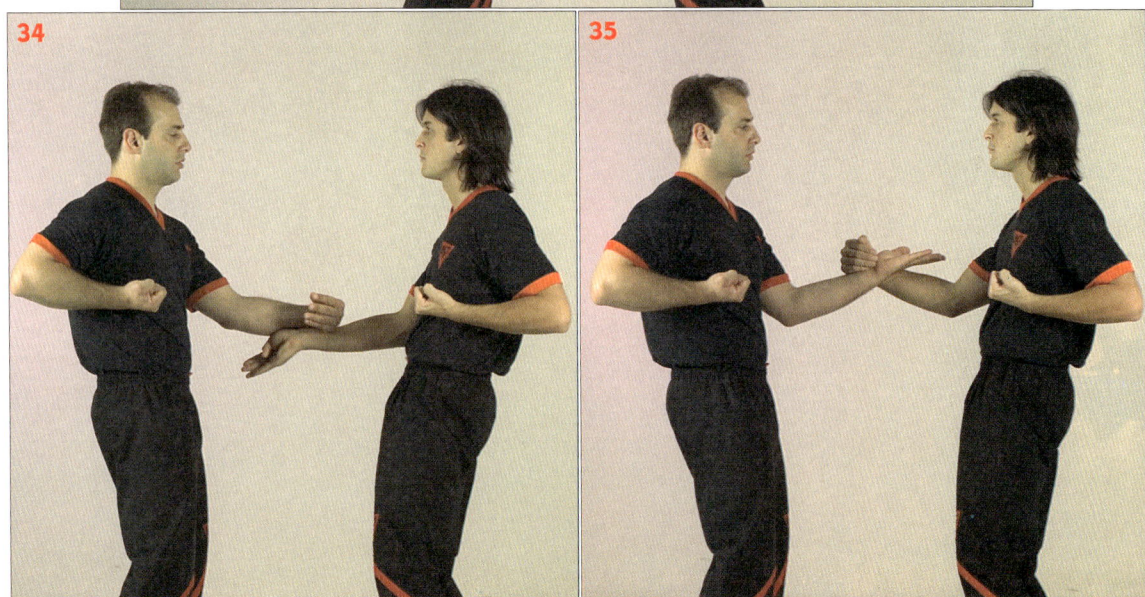

System 2
Tan Sao pushes outwards and Fook Sao way to it placing itself inside, **(pictures 36, 37, 38).**

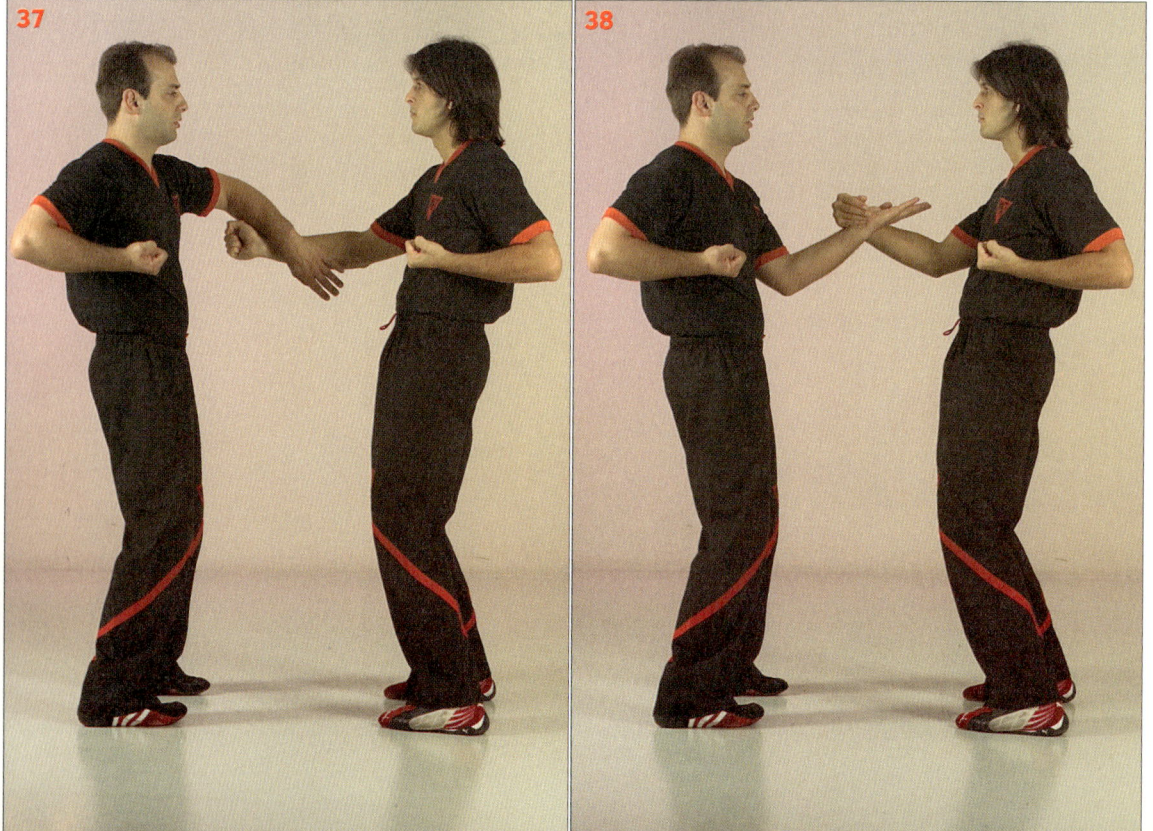

System 3

The fist pushes the Bong Sao downwards. Bong Sao gives way turning itself into a punch; at the same time, the former executes Bong Sao. Back to Fook-Tan position, exchanging roles.

Technical exercise

When students master the movements, they can pay more attention to sensations.

As a general rule, any gap should be used to point out mistakes committed by our partner, following the trial-error method explained above.

Hand changes or deliberate mistakes will be performed randomly in order to check that our partner is paying full attention and keeps the right pressure. Power and speed should be varied also as explained in the previous chapter. Exercises should be performed with both hands and rotating partners.

Introducing steps and turns

Once technical exercises are mastered, difficulty is increased by introducing steps and turns, thus starting development of qualities such as dynamic rooting or full-body co-ordination in punches and steps. Attacks will mainly be through the center in order to force a turn. Intensity and speed will vary according to the participant's will.

3rd Step: Poon Sao (rolling hands)

With Poon Sao, students start practicing Chi Sao with both arms simultaneously. Difficulty grows gradually as the student must pay attention to several zones at the same time (each arm individually, position and stance of the whole body).

Although Poon Sao may seem easy at first glance, it is absolutely not. It is structured in different stages or exercises.

Learning the movements
• Group 1: alternate techniques
Each student places his arms reversely, according to the following:

A (pictures 41, 42).

Tan Sao (right)
Fook Sao (left)

B (pictures 39, 40).

Fook Sao (left)
Bong Sao (right)

Fook Saos head the movement, as follows:
B pushes forwards with his Fook Sao, heading pressure to the center of A's body. A, for his part, gives way to him by performing Bong Sao **(pictures 43, 44)**.

At the same time, A's Fook Sao pushes forwards to make B's Bong Sao to absorb the energy, turning into Tan Sao **(pictures 43, 44)**.
This cycle is to be developed by making indefinite alternations.

- **Group 2: double techniques (pictures 45, 46).**

"A"	"B"
Bong Sao (right)	Fook Sao ((right)
Tan Sao (left)	Fook Sao (left)

In this exercise, one student attacks and the other absorbs.

Optionally, an instructor or higher-level student can train the student trough this exercise. Differences in technical level, especially in angles, pressure direction and sensitiveness, force the student to intensely correct the angles of his positions while keeping pressure. The result is exhausting; in just a few minutes arms fell extremely fatigued.

This is the reason why some students (and even instructors) call this exercise "the hell". After practicing this daily for a few weeks, great improvements in relaxation and technical correction are observed. Unconsciously, the student learns to use the right muscles with a minimum effort.

In any case, "the hell" is an exercise to be practiced through the entire life of the WT fighter. We can always improve practicing this exercise with someone on a higher level.

- **Group 3: changing hands (pictures 47, 48, 49)**

See this same group in the section describing one-hand Chi Sao.

- **Group 4: entering and opening**

Once a certain degree of technical correction is achieved, Chi Sao can be practiced in a more free way. Every gap is taken advance of, openings and feints are created in order to cause confusion in sensations, **(pictures 50, 51).**

Sifu Víctor Gutiérrez 77

- **Group 5: coordination exercises (pictures 52, 53, 54).**

Attacks and techniques are generated simultaneously with both arms, thus forcing the student to react individually with each one. This exercise helps develop the brain too! Complexity grows increasingly as the student progresses.

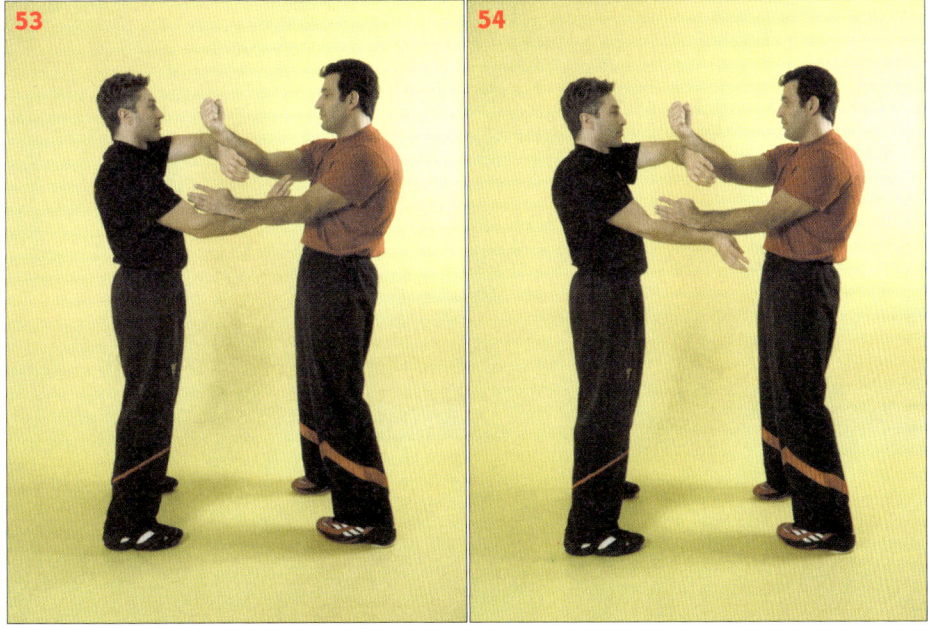

Most common mistakes

1. Fook Sao attack is too high so your partner can hit straight.
2. Fook Sao pushes downwards, so your partner lets it pass and responds with Fak Sao.
3. Bong Sao pressure direction is not correct, too focused on the hand, so your partner can pass below.
4. Pressure is lost in transition from Bong to Tan Sao; your partner can easily penetrate your guard.
5. When changing from Bong to Tan, pressure is headed outwards, so your partner can absorb the force using Kau Sao and then hit.
6. When passing from Tan Sao to palm-blow, the palm falls downwards or pushes outwards.
7. Fook Sao is not headed to the center, but in tangential direction, so Tan Sao advances with a palm or hand-side blow.

Sifu Víctor Gutiérrez 79

Free applications of Poom Sao

4th step: Chi Sao sections

This group of exercises has been developed by GM LEUNG TING for gradual learning of all WT concepts, as well as to increasingly fine-tune our coordination to reach the highest levels.

Here we introduce the first section, which embraces all Chi Sao subjects up to the 12th student grade. From the 12th student grade to the 1st technician grade, three more sections are learned. Each section is more advanced and complex than the previous one.

First section is the most important of all; it is the base to get the right inner sensations required to learn higher techniques. Each section is supported by the coordination and sensitiveness acquired in the previous section. New sections are aimed to rise such coordination and sensitiveness to a higher level of power and ability to absorb force. As a general guideline, we can say that, the higher the section trained, the closer the distance, the greater the explosiveness used and the more joints of the body simultaneously harmonized. The first section is the lowest, but it is the base, the foundation, and so, the most important section. The following attributes, among others, are trained:

1. Learning to grab and betray by giving way, without the opponent noticing the action (1st movement).
2. Learning to open gaps, without the opponent noticing it (1st movement).
3. Hitting coordinately with the step, so taking advance of the body-mass (various movements).
4. Absorbing the opponent's strength, accumulating potential energy with Passive Moving Turn and exploding in a punch thus transferring kinetic energy and offensive turn (3rd y 4th).
5. Increasing hitting power using the offensive Moving Turn (various movements).
6. Learning to keep stuck and relaxed when your opponent tries to push your arm aside by an explosive hand-blow (Pak Sao).
7. Learning to absorb explosive forces using turns in shorter distances (last bunch of movements).
8. Learning to develop power by coordinating muscle action of latissimus dorsi, scapulae and spinal erectors.
9. Introducing the crucial concept of bridge-hand, essential to penetrate a well-placed guard.

10. Intensively training passive and offensive turns and three of the four reactions - Kau Sao is excluded.

11. Working ambidexterity (separation of both arms coordination).

Starting the spring-mechanism work, which makes possible to absorb your opponent's force to the ground thus increasing your own stance stability.

DESCRIPTION OF THE FIRST SECTION

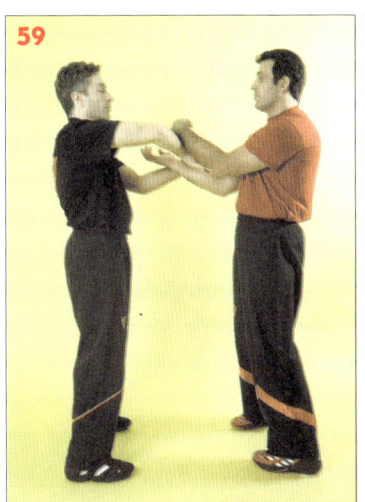

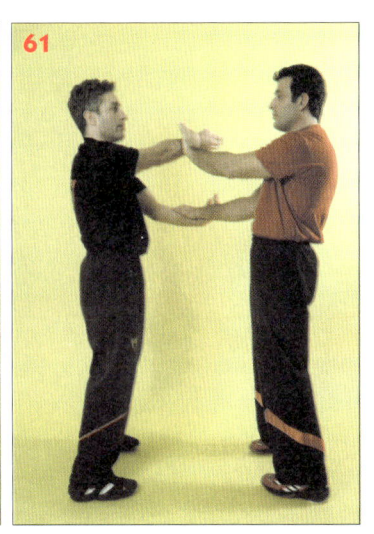

"A"= Sifu Javier Gutiérrez.
"B"= Sifu Víctor Gutiérrez.

Movement 1: Attack, "B" performs a Lop Sau (double trap and control plus palm-blow, **(pictures 59, 62).**

In **picture 62,** "B" reaches his target and steps in hitting "A".

In **pictures 65 and 66,** "B" gets in by attacking to "A"'s throat

Defense
"A" notices the attack and approach and gives way to it using right Lan Sau and left Chan, absorbing the attack with the Yin Elastic Energy.
So, "B" is forced to perform Bong Sau and left Pak Sau, **(pictures 63, 64).**

Counterattack
If "B" does not react with Bong and Pak or do it in excess or too late, a gap will be created through which "A" can counterattack, **(pictures 67, 68).**
Applying dynamic rooting and releasing Yang Elastic Energy accrued in the Yin movement.

Movement 2

"A", from the position in **picture 64,** in a movement of Yang Elastic Energy, attacks from the right side with a step.

"B" gives way with Bong Sau (turning with the Yin Elastic Energy) and Wu Sau, **(pictures 70, 70, 71).**

Counterattack

Releasing Yang Elastic Energy accrued in the Yin movement of Bong Wu, "B" counterattacks making "A" step back **(pictures 72, 73)** with an offensive turn.

MOVEMENT 3: BRIDGE-HAND

I Bridge-hand exercise, no footwork
"A" in right Bong and left Wu **(picture 74)**.
"B" in right bridge-hand, ready to cross the bridge with his left hand **(picture 74)**.
"B" attacks from left and crosses the bridge without a step forwards, **(pictures 75, 76)**.
"A" Counterattacks with left Wu Sau which after contacting, turns into a bridge-hand, **(pictures 77, 78)**. This forces "B" to turn his left punch into a Bong Sau to neutralize it **(picture 78)**.
Now, "A" attacks crossing the bridge without a step forwards this time, **(picture 79)**.

II Attack possibilities from bridge-hand (picture 80)

Picture 81: Right bridge-hand from "B" whose right punch crosses the bridge with a step forwards and hits "A"'s chest.

Picture 82: When "A" notices that bridge-hand succeeded, he quickly counterattacks with his left fist but "B", while hitting with left hand, gets back the right bridge-hand and places it on Wu Sau guard forming a wedge which neutralizes "A"'s left punch.

Picture 83: "A"'s Bong Sau lacks proper energy so "B"'s bridge-hand easily crosses the guard and traps "A"'s both hands.

Picture 84: "A"'s left hand defends with Wu Sau, thus neutralizing "B"'s attack deviating energy to the ground.

MOVEMENT 4: PAK SAU AND ATTACHED REACTIONS

III Bridge-hand BONG-WU- Turn
"B" attacks with his right bridge-hand and "A" gives way to him with his right Bong Sau, **(picture 85)**.
"B" crosses the bridge and throws a left punch.
"A" advances Wu Sau and makes contact **(picture 86)**.
"B" steps forwards and "A" gives way to him with Bong Wu and turn **(picture 87)**.

From the bridge-hand/punch movement explained above (pictures 88, 89), "A" launches a left punch which is neutralized by "B" by right Wu Sau-wedge **(picture 90)**. Then "B" performs left Pak Sau on "A"'s left arm **(picture 91)** then, "A"'s left arm gives way by left Bong Sau in order to neutralize "B"'s Pak Sau. At the same time, "B" is attacking with right punch through the gap created by Pak Sau **(picture 92)**. Simultaneously, "A" is transforming his Bong Sau in Wu Sau to neutralize "B"'s right punch **(picture 92)**. Two reaction possibilities are possible in this stance **(picture 92),** according to "B"'s attack.

First possibility
"B" attacks moving straight forwards. "A" gives way to him by turning in Bong-Wu. **(picture 93).**

Second possibility
"B" attacks with some upwards and/or outwards component (right, in this picture). "A" gives way with right Bong **(picture 94)** and simultaneously hits a straight-upwards (left) punch recto **(picture 95).**
"B" notices this later punch and gives way to it by going back and closing with right Cham-Sau **(picture 96).**

Third possibility
There is another. It is possible that, instead of reaching the position depicted in **picture 92,** "A"'s Wusau contacts in the inner part, not the outer. In this case **(pictures 97, 98)** "A" makes a Pak Sau on "B"'s attack. This is called Pak against Pak.
When "B" attacks with Pak Sau-punch **(picture 97)** "A" simultaneously defends and counterattacks with Pak Sau-punch **(pictures 98, 101).** Then "B", in turn, must move back with Bong-Wu, **picture 100 and picture 94** are the same with converse roles.

Fourth possibility
If "B"'s Pak Sau-punch is deficient "A" can counterattack with Wu Sau, like a wedge exploding forwards with Yang Elastic Energy **(pictures 105, 107)**, thus passing to right bridge-hand stance.

Combat applications of Pak Sau and attached reactions

Picture 108: From this attack on, several options are possible.
Picture 109: Left hand, which in **picture 108** hit, here makes Pak Sau thus clearing the way for a new right-hand blow, also trapping both arms.
Picture 110: "B" tries to defend by blocking the attack with right hand and/or right punch from "A" to the right.
"B" gives way by right Bong Sau (punch turns into Bong Sau when "B"'s defense is noticed, thus clearing the way for a left punch **(picture 111)**.
Pictures 112, 113: "B" defends forwards. "A" gives way to him with Lop Sau (grips) and hits simultaneously.

Movement 5:
Bong-Wu against Gaun-punch

Pictures 114, 115, 116 show the well-known sequence of "B" attacking with Pak Sau-punch and "A" counterattacking with Bong Wu.

Then, "B"'s right fist contacts right Wu Sau which turns into a Bong Sau to open a gap **(picture 117)**.

"A" takes advantage of this gap and attacks with a left punch. But "B" notices this and close the path with Cham Sau **(picture 118)**.

"A"'s energy is properly headed and supported with a forward step, so "B" must give way with a turn **(picture 119)**.

"A" notices that his punch failed and immediately transforms it into Bong Sau **(picture 119)**.

"B" counterattacks with Gaun Sau-punch which destroys "A"'s Bong forcing him to perform Wu-Sau, **(picture 120)**.

"B" notices "A"'s Wu Sau-wedge and adapts his punch to neutralize and pass it changing the angle with an offensive turn, thus forcing "A" to give way in Bong-Wu plus turn to avoid the blow **(picture 121)**.

"B" performs left Gaun Sau to open "A"'s Bong and attack with right punch **(picture 122)**.

Again, "B" turns and changes the attack angle. "A" turns Wu Sau into Bong Sau **(pictures 123, 124)**. In this case the sequence is performed in the right side, while in **picture series 119, 120, 121** it was left side. This way, both sides can be alternated indefinitely.

Some combat applications are described below, starting in **picture 125** stance, with two options.

In these movements it is very important to use the "fall" of bodyweight in steps and turns to achieve explosive power.

94 The Tao of the action

CHAPTER V
Fundamentals and methods of power training

WT requires, as explained in chapter III "How to learn", a specific "science" to combine maximum economy of movement and hitting power. Follows a breakdown, by sections, of mechanisms intervening in this process:

1. Angles to apply force.
2. The turn.
3. The trigger principle (forwards pressure).
4. Full-body coordination.
5. The spring principle.
6. Lowering your gravity center.
7. Using weight and inertia.
8. Relaxation.
9. Active stretching.
10. Muscle control.
11. Continuous burst.

1. Angles to apply force

WT follows a general principle: every technique has a rooting component. This means that you should always feel like pushing the floor with the weight of your body. To achieve this, among other things, shoulders must be pulling downwards at all times. If shoulders rise, they lose their "root"; balance cannot be maintained and strong blows are hardly possible. For instance, straight punches in WT have a double aim: to de-root your opponent and increase your own support on the floor when you punch. This is possible due to the angle of your arm combined with the right muscle tensions. This extent is analyzed in the front stance and the step forward stance. We see three people pushing Sifu Víctor's arms without arriving to move him. Sifu placed his arms in an angle where all pressure received is transferred through the triangle formed by his arms towards his belly, pelvis and legs, thus securing him more firmly to the ground. To achieve this effect, latissimus dorsi, scapulae, transverse abdominals, obliques, serratus and rectus abdominis muscles coordinate acting as a spring, adjusting direction and pressure.

On **picture 131** a straight punch to the chest in adduction stance is showed. If we look at it from the side, power angles can be observed. Impact reaction will create a straight descending line towards Sifu Víctor's body, pushing him against the ground thus conferring him greater stability. If elbow is placed outside, force is headed outwards, it does not find Victor's body mass support. On the contrary, if elbow is placed inside, the body is placed on the back, so the blow is launched with the support of his whole body mass.

Some experts not knowing WT consider that the adduction stance provides lateral stability but lacks frontal stability (B. Lee's Fighting Method no. 2), as they understand this stance in the light of its potential technical application to other styles, ignoring specific WT biomechanics. Front stance is very stable if you know how to direct your enemy's energy to the ground passing through his own body. This skill requires using the right angles and moving your joints in a coordinated fashion like springs (this subject will be dealt with below).

Now we will deal with punches from the step forward stance. This stance is even more powerful, as the power line hammers the rear leg on the floor, taking advance of its drive.

Two types of punches can be distinguished here:

• Punch from the same side as the advanced leg., **(picture 132)**.

• Punch from the same side as the rear leg, **(picture 133)**.

132

133

Connection is similar, however it is more obvious when the punch comes from the same side as the rear leg.

In any case, WT attacks are performed in continuous punch bursts, so it requires a permanent support system, regardless the rear leg is in the same side as the punching hand. This support system can be achieved in a front stance, with no rotation of shoulders.

As explained below -when the steps system is tackled in detail-, the front stance is aimed to transfer force, from both hips and the back, supported by inertia from the step, to both hands simultaneously; so, you can punch with both hands. This is one of the main reasons why shoulders should not be turned.

All in all, the triangular structures outlined by the power transfer lines as showed in **picture 134** form a cone or pyramid of kinetics whose base is the body of the WT fighter, and whose vertex is one or two points in the opponent's central line. The pyramid base is laid down on the ground due to its bottom-up lean.

Triangles in the drawing should not be construed as fixed forms. Their sides are flexible like elastic springs stretched and compressed to modify proportions between one side and the others. This way, maximum rooting of your own body is achieved, directing received pressure to the ground and stepping on it to project the same energy.

An important detail is that, at the time of the impact, the arm is not fully stretched out. The hit must occur in an intermediate point of the punch route. If the arm is fully stretched out, the angle forming its power vector would be horizontal, not oblique **(picture 135)** so it would not connect so effectively with pelvis and legs. If the arm is fully stretched out, power would be less, as its support by the body is diminished. This is another reason that makes it necessary to place the arm in an intermediate phase of the extension-penetration. Under this circumstances, the arm goes on stretching out some inches, thus unbalancing the enemy. When you punch, you should imagine that your hand passes through the opponent to reach a point located just behind him. This adds power and inertia.

Although the opponent is unbalanced backwards, WT continuous steps keep you stuck to him, and punches in continuous burst multiply this effect maintaining him in permanent instability.

2. The moving turn

The bodyweight moving turns notably increase power in short distance. As explained above, passive turn absorbs your opponent's energy and accumulates it under the form or potential energy, just like when you compress a spring.

When the attack is surpassed, the spring triggers, releasing its power. Additionally, the power of hitting in Moving Turn has other effects. An important weight passage occurs, providing a sharp increase in power **(see pictures 136).** The extent of this increase depends on the turn being performed in full or partial round.

Moving Turn se can be used in different ways:
• Partial Moving Turn in straight punch (palm or fist).
• Full Moving Turn in straight punch.
• The same variations in hits from different angles:
  • Round punch.
  • Upward elbow.
  • Downward elbow.
  • Low palm.
  • Upward punch (uppercut-type).
  • Downward pressure (Gwat Sao in turn, last part of the 1st section).
Moving Turn + step forward (power is multiplied when the step is added).

3. The trigger principle (forwards pressure)

As explained above, all movements have a forward pressure component (towards the center of the enemy, following the central line concept). Without this pressure, WT is rendered totally ineffective. The higher the WT level, the lower the pressure exerted, so the more difficult for your enemy to feel your movements.

The trigger principle uses two kinesiology laws:
1ª) If you stretch a muscle first, it will contract more powerfully. This is a very popular -although widely misused- principle.

Some mistake its application to athletics for its Martial Arts use. For instance, javelin launchers fully stretch their arm backwards to open the chest and shoulder (previous stretch) and so achieve more efficiency. However, this kind of movement is not advisable if the aim is to improve combat skills. Arms would be required to open in excess, so announcing every punch, in which case your opponent could crush you at will.

You should not pre-stretch big muscles (chest, back, etc.), but the shorter ones (hip rotators, rotator cuffs). That is exactly what we do when giving way to a force. Some examples follow:
- If you give way using Bong Sao, you stretch your external rotator cuff and triceps. Just like in Kao Sao and Cham Sao.
- When you give way in other techniques, there is a micro-flexion in the backbone, produce of a stretching in the short paravertebral muscles. Legs and hips are also flexed slightly.
- Muscles require a previous muscle tone in order to contract quickly and powerfully. If a muscle is totally relaxed, it must be activated before contacting.

This is activation tone. This tone is provided by forwards pressure. You can do this test:
- Choose a partner and place you both according.
- First, relax your arm totally. Now, without prior warning, your partner retires his palm and you have to launch a punch as fast as possible.
- Repeat the same process but, this time, start pushing slightly your partner's hand from the beginning. Just a little bit; the minimum pressure required to feel, without shoving his hand.
- Repeat the experiment this way now.
- Your fist is launched more quickly and powerfully.
- Activation tone is limited. If you overdo, your partner would feel it and take advance of your strength.
- Forwards pressure is important for other reason.

In traditional methods, you draw back your arm immediately after punching. This draw-back creates a "gap" which can be used by your opponent to penetrate your guard. In WT, the opposite principle is applied: you keep stuck. However, this principle loses effectiveness if there is no pressure forwards. Without forwards pressure there are hardly no difference between drawing back your hand and keeping it stuck.

4. Full-body coordination

Este apartado es difícil de descubrir, ya sea por escrito o con imágeThis subject is difficult to explain, whether in writing or graphically. In fact, only through years of regular and correct practice one can understand the real meaning of "using your full body ". Here we can just outline some general basics for any individual student to "seek" during practice.

First of all, it is necessary to describe which are the most important muscles for this purpose and which muscles must remain passive in WT movements.

Frequently unknown, the main muscles giving power to arm WT techniques are:

LATISSIMUS DORSI with synergic action (muscular contraction supporting and perfecting other muscle action) from anterior serratus, obliques, transverse abdominal and rectus abdominal muscles. They produce a downwards force vector which contributes to rooting and shoulder relaxation. Certain muscle fibers (side and inferior) from pectoral take part in this movement

Now see how this works in a straight punch.

Imagine glenohumeral (shoulder) joint as a pulley. Action of all those muscles (A) induces rotation (B). We can take advance of this rotation component if we know how to add it to other muscle groups actions projecting their vectors forwards (C). The aforementioned muscles (back, anterior serratus, obliques, transverse abdominal, rectus abdominal and pectoral muscles) are among the biggest muscles of your body, so they can create a great deal of force.

Muscle system in the scapular waist:
There are two groups of actions.
• External rotation (to which latissimus dorsi lowering etc. is added).
• Passage (anterior antepulsion). Consists on the forwards displacement following the arm's stretch-out movement.

Important

External rotation, antepulsion should not be accompanied by turn Antepulsion in the scapular waist.

External rotation effect
Collar bones and thoracic cavity maintain front position and symmetry while scapula slides forwards.

To gain an impression of how does it work, stand up and lean your back against a wall, adopting WT stance. Then, trying to keep the back, especially the dorsal area (between both scapulae), stuck to the wall and try to stretch out arms and shoulders forwards at maximum, sliding scapulae over the thoracic cavity. This is scapular antepulsion or passage.

Try the same but, first of all, turn your shoulder back, out and down (rotation, extension + lowering) through the action of latissimus dorsi and other muscles. Then add scapulae passage (fo 2). Stretch your arm forwards in a continuous fashion, just like if you wanted to split your joints. (contraction of triceps and anconeus, and active stretching of tendons with "decoaptation")

Differentiation of joints - shoulder, elbow, wrist). (DRAWING) Fist must be relaxed at all times.

Muscles of scapular waist are very important. This can be easily established through the following test: lean your back against a wall as showed in. Ask one or several persons stronger than you to try to avoid that you separate your scapulae from the wall. No matter how hard they push, you will easily defeat them. However, the coordination process described above is more complex than it looks. People without WT training, when performing passage or antepulsion of scapulae, they tend to rise shoulders, contracting trapezius and angling shoulder blades or rotating shoulders internally using major and minor pectoralis muscles. This movement is totally ineffective, as disconnects arm and shoulder from trunk and legs, thus preventing the use of spinal, dorsal and abdominal muscles, as well as leg muscles associated to those in the scapular waist and the arm.

So, in WT these muscle groups must be used with a different pattern: instead of antepulsion + inner rotation + shoulder rise, in WT we have outwards rotation + lowering + antepulsion; so the scapular waist is connected to the backbone (paravertebral muscles) and pelvis (through latissimus dorsi and the diagonal chain comprised of anterior serratus + obliques + transverse abdominal + rectus abdominal), and through the pelvis to the lower members, whose muscles are so powerful.

Paravertebral muscle system (spinal extensors)
This is another fundamental and very powerful group. In the execution of a straight high punch, backbone makes a short extension, a micro-movement, however essential. This extension presents particular subtleties. Between muscles extending (paravertebrals) and flexing the backbone (abdominals) a series of paradoxical actions and reactions are to occur, in which diaphragm (respiratory muscle separating abdominal cavity from thoracic cavity) is also involved. This actions and reactions are paradoxical because, although the functions of these muscles are opposite (extension vs. flexion) they are to act in a single movement, when a sort of internal wave will be transferred through the raquis to the scapular waist.

Lower extremities muscles
1. External hip rotators (gluteus, piriform, etc.)
2. Approximators. (adductors, pectineus, internal rectus)
3. Knee extensors (quads).
4. Ankle flexors (sural triceps: calves and soleus).
5. Plantar flexors.

Between the groups 1 and 2, some paradoxical actions are to occur too.

Lower extremities, as a whole, will perform an extension micro-movement, continuing in the backbone wave. It is worth to note the adduction pressure (approximation) between both thighs, simultaneous to anteversion movement in the pelvis, opposite in nature. Adductor muscles connect legs and abs through pubic symphysis, which external hip rotators (gluteus and piriform) connect legs and spinal extensors. These two systems are involved in the paradoxical action-reaction function of raquis flexors and extensors. Their relevance to unite the body in one neuromuscular unit is maximum.

Finally, imagine each joint-muscle system as a relay where kinetics is accelerated through a minimum extension-rotation movement (micro-movement, in fact).

So, we have 7 acceleration points.

In fact, every vertebra would be a cog.

However, in the interests of convenience, we consider them all together as point 5:
1. Foot plant.
2. Ankle.

3. Knee.
4. Hip – Pelvis.
5. Backbone.
6. Scapular waist.
7. Elbow

This seven areas are to be coordinated to form one single shockwave by means of the paradoxical action of trunk flexors and extensors and leg approximators and separators.

Anyway, you should bear in mind that we are discovering how does a WT expert's body work, not an student's.

Another important aspect is that we are analyzing living processes which cannot be separated actually, as they occur in a virtually simultaneous way. So, for instance, a punch goes forwards at the same time the rest of the mechanisms are activated, not afterwards. All written descriptions are hardly futile for those who do not have the relevant practice level, but they can improve learning for those who are already working on it

5. The spring principle and force absorption

In the first part of this book, we anticipated that the spring principle acts just like the ABS device in a car: braking, diminishing your enemy's power.

This section explains how does it work. To this end, the study should be divided in two parts:

Biomechanics: Force-absorption lines

In order to absorb force, WT unites a complete network of proprioceptive connections in the shape of triangles. Through these triangles, absorbed force is directed to the ground. Exercises in the Chi Sao sections help to gradually develop these proprioceptive connections.

In this drawing, arms are not taken into account, but they also establish two main connection lines:
Elbow - scapular waist
Elbow - pelvis (in Tan Sao), **(picture 137).**

An expert would consciously feel how the micro-movement he performs to absorb a punch from his opponent conducts kinetics through his arm - scapular waist - backbone - pelvis - leg and foot to the ground in a second. The more developed the proprioceptive connections the lesser the movement required to absorb the force. Finally, we arrive at micro-movements which are not perceptible with the naked eye. For instance, if an expert enters the guard and hits a punch burst, only a burst of straight punches can be seen from the outside. Possibly, in the route of some of those punches there are several micro-movements aimed to absorb the reaction force of the opponent's arms. This micro-movements enable to enter the enemy's guard while controlling his arms simultaneously. This happens in a range of 1 or 2 millimeters; imperceptible for the human eye.

Follows a description of some simple force-transmission lines:

Example: BONG SAO + TURN. Passage, (picture 138).

138

El Bong Sao is the most complex movement in WT. It consists of inner rotation + lowering + scapular antepulsion + elbow rise.

By nature of human body, if your shoulder rotates internally and the elbow rises, trapezius and middle deltoid contract, thus rising the shoulder. But Bong Sao combines inner rotation and dorsal contraction in order to the shoulder comes down, instead of rising.

Through this downwards movement, the shoulder gets connected through latissimus dorsi with the same side's pelvis and hip. The opponent's force is transferred through the arm to the shoulder, where it gets connected to the hip which makes it go out, placing the bodyweight on that leg, making the moving turn and bodyweight passage thanks to the adduction pressure which always exists between both legs in all WT stances, dragging it to the opposite leg and turning the foot putting heel inside. The turn is completed. Feet push firmly to the ground and absorb energy towards it.

Example 2. Tan Sao and Moving Turn

This time, connection line is different: Force is transferred from shoulder to the opposite hip through the shoulder-opposite hip diagonal line. Right shoulder goes down and rotates outwards, pushing the opposite left hip outwards so dragging knee and ankle to the left through the adduction force between both legs, thus making heel to rotate inwards.

Muscles are springs

Now, additionally to those transmission lines, imagine there is a full system of springs inside them, which compress progressively as the force passes through these springs. Thanks to this system, a very short range is required to absorb force, rendering the moving turn almost unnecessary.

Muscles are springs. When you give way to a force, your muscles should stretch, not in a passive fashion but through a stretching with progressive and force-proportional eccentric contraction. This contraction is merely forwards pressure, always present in WT movements. Muscles involved are all those in the transmission iine (scapular waist, backbone, hips, legs). As explained above, when you hit, each body segment produces acceleration. When you give way to a force, the reverse mechanism is applied - each segment delivers deceleration.

Through this system, kinesiology mechanisms required to increase force are achieved: previous stretching. In this case it is a microstretching performed by many muscles at a time, which makes up for the short width of the stretching.

Activation tone: merely pressure forwards, responsible for progressive and adaptive eccentric contraction.

In this way, when force is absorbed, potential energy is accumulated. This energy will proportional to the spring compression, to the extensor and rotator muscles stretching, in fact.

Potential energy becomes kinetics when the attack is surpassed.

詠 春 拳

6. Lowering your gravity center

Certain techniques take maximum benefit of your latissimus dorsi and abdominal strength through an explosive short lowering of your gravity center combined with a slight shrug of your body. The power achieved through this movement can be increased by associating it to a moving turn:
• Top-down elbow with turn **(picture 139).**

- Round punch, **(picture 140).**

140

- Side Fak Sao **(picture 141).**

Scapular waist is pushed down coordinately with a slight backbone flexion.

Lowering your gravity center in straight punches.

Straight punches below the inferior of half of the breastbone limit are not performed through extension, as above, but flexion and body lowering.

This is the case, for instance, for a straight punch to the lower part of the breast bone or the stomach (or both at a time, in double-punch), a palm-blow to kidneys or liver area.

These techniques take advantage of your bodyweight. You let it fall and accelerate this force through the coordinated contraction of big muscle groups such as:

- **Arm:** triceps, anconeus, vertical wrist flexo.
- **Scapular waist:** external rotator cuff, teres minor, sub-scapular shoulder antepulsors, major pectoralis.
- **Trunk:** latissimus dorsi, anterior serratus, transverse abdominal muscles, rectus abdominal; go down the shoulder and flex the trunk.
- **Pelvis flexor and legs:** gluteus, rear thigh (biceps femoris, semi-tendinous, semimembranous etc.)
- **Legs:** Triceps femoris (calves, soleus), when you take the sole of the foot as a fixed point, these muscles act as knee flexors. Tibialis anterior and peroneus: antagonists of triceps femoris. They push the sole of the foot against the floor thus enabling knee flexion from triceps femoris.
- **Diaphragm:** acts as a compressor pump in combination with serratus and intercostals.

As we can see here, very big and powerful muscle groups are at stake. This explains the power achieved in the "one-inch punch" **(picture 142)** or even "zero-inch-punch" in adduction front position, feet in parallel, with no turn in shoulders.

Power is increased when bodyweight moving turn and / or a short step forward is added. Or just the leg-forward stance.

This kind of blows are extremely powerful although their range is minimum. In any case, a difference must me established between one-inch punches displayed in exhibitions and the real one-inch punch:

- One-inch punches displayed in exhibitions makes the person receiving them to move back several meters. It is spectacular how such an effect can be achieved with hardly no movement. However,

this punch is not much effective, as causes no significant injury to the person being punched. Most of the energy is lost when hurling him in the air.
  • The real one-inch punch does not significantly displaces the recipient but it will cause serious damage to him; frequently he falls struck down to the ground. In this case, all energy is absorbed by the recipient's body. He takes the whole shockwave so his internal organs can be damaged. If it is applied on the breastbone, it is easy for the heart to bear the blow, as it is protected by the ribcage.
   This kind of punch is not easy to master, but its usefulness and danger are maximum.

142

7. Using weight and inertia

Kinesiology mechanisms studied heretofore can be combined with WT steps or initial burst thus multiplying its efficiency. If you just perform the starting step correctly, a great deal of energy is created. The reason is that WT steps move the whole body, with full support from both hips and backbone, fully forwards "passing through" the enemy. The step does not finish when contacting; it keeps on penetrating. As bodyweight is maintained in the rear leg, advance is continuous and direction can be varied at any time.

8. Relaxation

When hitting on relaxed fists, not clenching them, all kinetics is transferred to the enemy's body. This way, fists also adapt to the surface.

9. Active stretching

In straight punches, the arm tries to continuously stretch out, like aiming to split the bones forming the joints in a straight direction, into space. This increases power and prevents injury when performing punches in the air; there is not a lock or limit for joints.

Indeed, stretching when training antagonist muscles (i.e. flexors) improves hitting power as peripheral resistance to movement are reduced.

10. Muscle control

In order to get maximum power and speed in any given movement, agonist muscles must contract at maximum while antagonists are fully relaxed. Learning this is essential, and it is one of the benefits of forms.

11. Continuous burst

WT advocates for fluid and permanent attack. Any trained individual can be able to launch bursts of 5 punches per second. Expert WT fighters can even achieve 10 punches per second.

Advantages of continuous punch burst are numerous.
- It causes stunning in the opponent's nervous system through saturation, preventing him of deciding response.
- When you are given a blow, your body contracts for a second, and the relaxes. In this relaxation phase you are most vulnerable. Hitting in a continuous burst takes advantage of the relaxation phase to cause even greater harm.
- Hits are given in the same point, so each new punch causes more injury.

Sifu Víctor Gutiérrez 117

Sifu Javier Gutiérrez

3rd PART
Self-Defense

CHAPTER I
WT Applied to Self-Defense

No doubt, why Self-Defense?

Self-Defense, I.E. the ability to defend oneself from physical aggression without any weapon, was the lure and attraction for the public when Eastern martial arts started to become popular. At the beginning, it was the Japanese, of low height, expert in Jiu-Jitsu, who were capable of crushing hefty Europeans or Americans apparently with no effort. Then Bruce Lee appeared, and Kung Fu and Karate movies displaying one single empty-handed man overwhelmed a gang of six or more armed rowdies. What impressed audience so much? Obviously, it was the individual power feeling, the chance to overcome even the most impossible obstacles depicted in those pictures. Self-confidence and energy displayed by those characters fascinated (and in some extent they still fascinate) uncountable people.

However, the Asian fighter myth was exaggerated to excess and in recent times it has been increasingly deflated to the point of even being ridiculed in many films. Action movies are still popular, but the audience is not so gullible. People watch those films as entertainment, being conscious that everything is fantasy, just like James Bond pictures.

But what happened to all those enthusiastic people going to a gym to learn Self-Defense? What did they find? Certain exoticism sometimes, and a huge deal of sport and very little Self-Defense.

In the light of this situation, there were movements for going back to the origins. So, systems exclusively devoted to Self-Defense were thus created o recovered.

In any case, it is easy to confirm some facts:
1. Only a small percentage of students take part in tournaments.
2. The rest attend WT classes for any of the following reasons:
- Self-Defense.
- Fitness.
- Social relations.
- Cultural or philosophical reasons.
- Health improvement.

3. It is totally compatible to improve physical condition while training Self-Defense exercises

4. As no competition exist between students, Self-Defense focus of classes favors social relations.
5. Martial arts philosophy is related to the openness of real combat, with no rules.

So, technical focus on Self-Defense is more adequate for a vast majority of students than taking them to the sports path.

This is the reason why WT Leung Ting system is a traditional Kung Fu style on which Self-Defense is emphasized.

WT's specific features also fully engage each other in order to achieve good Self-Defense skills, as explained below.

Here we try to analyze all factors involved in a Self-Defense situation, with the aim of understanding how WT training makes you capable of solving it. Five main factors must be studied in analyzing the victim of an aggression.

1. Psychological factors

Serenity and self-confidence are the qualities which ideally should dominate when you suffer an aggression. However, this only happen exceptionally, unless a specific training has been followed. On a regular basis, fear is the first reaction. This fear would vary according to how impressionable you are and how aggressive and strong your enemy looks.

Fear

Fear, for itself, is not bad. Problems arise when fear makes you freeze or be prey of hysteria. It is crucial to channel fear towards a smart response.

In WT, this smart response is the first thing you learn; the so-called "Universal solution": It consists in heading to the central line of your opponent with both arms and a kick forming a protective wedge around your vital points at the same time you hit. Advancing towards the attacker, psychologically means that you have no fear, and obliges him to pass to a defensive stance. Kick-start forwards is effected when the enemy enters the so-called "critical distance", as explained in further detail in the training system section.

It is important to understand the psychological effect of applying the universal solution in a Self-Defense situation. Aggressor, who started in a superiority position, who was going to intimidate his victim, is taken by surprise when his prey not only does not move back in fear but also comes down on him in a continuous blow burst. Now he is in danger; he has to defend himself and feels fear. Victim comes to a dominant position and sees how his self-confidence rises. A complete reversion of the situation has taken place.

If fear is trust's enemy, serenity has no less dangerous enemies:

Pride, la imprudence and anger. Fear's antipodes can place you in an unnecessary dangerous situation. How? Reacting to banal provocations with violence, thus falling in exhibitionism or fighting when it is better to run.

What can we say about those ridiculous fights for traffic arguments or a shove in a disco?

If you are calmed, you would be able to assess the situation with the required objectivity and, in case there is a way to peacefully solve the dispute, take it. If action is the only way, keeping cold blood is even more necessary.

Traditionally, there was a rule to "not display Kung Fu in public". This rule served several purposes: Keeping techniques in secret, surprising the aggressor and avoiding getting in trouble. The idea was to go unnoticed, that nobody could suspect that you practiced Kung Fu. A very muscular look was sometimes counterproductive -- "smaller" enemies could be dissuaded, but maybe they would be led to attack in group or to use weapons more dangerous than usual. A perfect example of "hidden power" was great master Leung Lan Kwai. Even his family not knew he was a WT expert until he once intervened to defend a man being hit by a group of attackers.

It is pretty obvious that we have greatly forgotten this rule. Certainly, times change and danger is not "just around the corner". However, from a psychoanalysis viewpoint, it is worthwhile to wonder why do we use t-shirts, jackets, trousers, stickers or pins with drawings or logos allusive to this gym or the other or a martial art? Why do we joke with our friends displaying our skills, especially if they are girls? Is it a marketing strategy to attract new students? How much is true and how much is insecurity?

Surprise factor

This is a really powerful, often decisive, element. Very often, surprise works in the aggressor's favor, as he chooses the moment for the attack. But it also can be on the victim's side, if he/she reacts in an unexpected way. An apparently "inoffensive" person will have more chances to catch the attacker unawares if he uses Self-Defense techniques than some one with "strong" look or who "appears knowing some martial arts". It is also true that a 5.25 ft. tall 120 lbs. guy has more chances of suffering an assault than a 6.30 ft. Mr. Olympia -- crooks are not silly. However, there are not many Olympias out there, and most of us seem "not so dangerous" at first sight, so it is better to have surprise factor on our side.

All in all, whether for gaining a certain tactical advantage or for preventing getting in trouble, it is advisable to cultivate a middling look.

Also, in order to minimize the chance of being taken by surprise, it would be advisable to develop a state of "INTENSIFIED ATTENTION AND ALERTNESS" just as Buddhism proposes -- live the present moment with lucidity and wisdom. Instead of thinking about one thing or the other, when walking down the street you should be conscious of your stance and gravity center; open your senses to your environment. An extra benefit of paying attention to the present without judging what you perceive is the calmness achieved by banishing stress for ever. This is not easy in today's society, but you can try even when you will not reach the levels achieved by ancient times samurais

Impressionability

This is another psychological facet which should be borne in mind. If you are to "scare" someone, which should be the most appropriate look? Impeccable suit, well neat, good manners and a smile on your face? Of course not. On the contrary, burliness, scars, tattoos, three days' stubble, serious stance and flashy clothes, combined with aggressive talk and "psycho" face would be the ideal look to IMPRESS. Everybody knows this. That is why they use such an image.

Training must teach you to overcome this "impression". Certain psychological techniques are really useful for this purpose. Our own

Sifu Víctor Gutiérrez 123

Surprise factor

STANCE AND BODY LANGUAGE should not be forgotten either. According to the circumstances, it can be more useful to adopt a greater or lesser power attitude in order to dissuade or surprise.

2. Physical factors

Here we tackle physical factors such as height, weight, sex, strength, stamina, suppleness, speed and pain tolerance.

Self-Defense only requires average qualities to work. If you are above the average, it is better for your health and for anything you want to do. If you are below the average, your qualities will be improved with training.

3. Technical factors

Controlling the opponent's movements

There is a law in empty-hand combat -- the shorter the distance, the greater control over the opponent. Regarding hits, closing distance is the best way to cancel out most of any opponent's "arsenal". Just watch an English boxing, Kick Boxing or Muay Thai fight. When a boxer wants to avoid his opponent's blows, he leaves his arms stuck to his and comes close to him. This way, he controls the opponent's arms, if they move, he notices and hold them using his own arms.

WT developed this tactic to its logical conclusion. However, for these techniques to work out it is necessary to learn to hit in a very short distance using hands and feet. Hence the idea of "stickiness" characterizing our style. If you cross hands with a WT expert, the feeling you get is to be overwhelmed and trapped in a sort of straitjacket. It seems you are unable to move, there is a shower of blows and you feel you lose balance and cannot recover it.

WT expert passes from long to the shortest distance with amazing ease thanks to Chi Sao, while continuously hitting at the same time. His ideal distance is the one in which he fully controls his opponent and he can apply 100% of his blows. That is to say, shoulders and chest at a forearm's distance (ex the hand). In this distance, 100% of kicks and punches are avoided. Regarding hits with elbow and knee, grappling or projections, they are prevented by the stickiness of arms and legs.

So there are four elements which are essential to succeed:

Closing distance
Stickiness   = Victory guaranteed
Sensitiveness
Short-hitting ability

This formula avoids all unforeseen or surprise factors in a fight, which is essential for Self-Defense because it is always an unpredictable situation. the only chance for the aggressor is to knock you out before you notice him.

Spontaneous movements

You do not know from where or how you will be attacked, so any preconceived idea or techniques scheme will not be very useful. The key is to adapt yourself, like water adapts to the shape of its recipient, to any circumstances without needing to think or decide. In WT there is a universal solution: head to the center of your opponent continuously hitting and creating a protective wedge. This movement is valid for any situation. The whole training consist on applying the universal solution and spontaneously adapting to the enemy's forces. You must learn to wait until your opponent enters the critical distance and to not react to feints he would do outside this distance.

Re-educate instinctive inadequate reactions is one of the purposes of this exercise -- avoiding to close your eyes, moving back or turning your arms away. At the beginning, training should be performed little by little. Then, greater difficulty should be introduced gradually in order to develop unconscious adaptability: punches, kicks, grappling, projection attempt, feints and complex attack combinations. The student limits himself to perform the universal solution and tries to relax in order to give way and adapt to obstacles. Step by step, the student learns to flow without thinking and "letting things flourish by themselves" applying sensitiveness. However, he may be taken by surprise and find himself in a closed distance situation. Here is where "sticky sensitiveness " training is most useful. An advanced WT fighter will find his body reacting and opening gaps unconsciously and, almost without even noticing, he would have responded successfully. In the first part of this book "TAO IN ACTION" we explained the meaning and the training of "adaptability" so we will not repeat it here.

126 The Tao of the action

A rote learning of techniques will always present two faults -- lack of spontaneity and excess of slowness. The only way to overcome these problems is training sensitiveness applied to combat.

To sum up, instead of learning "Self-Defense techniques", in WT only one technique is learnt -- universal solution-- and only one thing must be progressed on --improving sensitiveness to gain adaptability. Inner sensitiveness (conscience of own mind and body) and outer sensitiveness (perception of the partner(s) and the environment).

Sifu Víctor Gutiérrez 127

CHAPTER II
Self-Defense against multiple attacks

Here is a great myth of martial arts. Is it possible to come through a group aggression unscathed?

Some answer "no", thus leaving their students without any option. Their argument is "is it possible to defeat two opponents as skilful as you?" Answer to this question is obviously no. So they conclude it is useless trying to overcome a multiple attack. But this question is nothing but a trap.

The conclusion reached is not true. Following the same pattern, one could wonder: "Would you be able to defeat someone more skilful than you?" Answer is obviously no, as if your opponent is, by definition, better than you, it means he is going to win. So, following the same reasoning, the following conclusion would be drawn: "As I am never going to defeat someone more skilful than me, why would I bother to learn a martial art? I should better devote my time to fitness."

But the question can be varied: "Could you defeat two or three opponents LESS skilful than you?" The answer is different, right? It is open -maybe or maybe not. Experience shows that some fighters have been aggressed by three or more attackers and prevailed and others, unfortunately, not.

But this does not mean that it is going to be always like this.

If you are taken by surprise, chances are scarce, virtually nil. If the group is numerous and they can attack simultaneously, you are totally lost. If they are expert fighters or have weapons, the only option is to run away, and even this option is not always available.

In fact, the first and best thing to decide in any situation of group attack is to run away.

There are too many risks. But, what if the way out is cut off?

Your chances of success will depend on your expertise, on your degree of superiority in relation to your attackers and on the use of the right strategy.

This is what we train for; to be better, much better than any rook. Do you think that aggressors you can find in the street are super class fighters like Mirko CroCop or Minotauro? Not at all. Main objective in self-defense in a group attack: open a hollow to escape successfully.

You cannot knock out 3 or 5 people. Your only objective is to escape unscathed; no more and no less. So, you should try to stun them or render them useless in order to run away.

Strategy: Stay in the periphery of a virtual circle formed by the attacking group so they have to encounter each other. Use your enemy's bodies as shields and barriers **(pictures 143 to 150).**

145
146
147
148
149
150

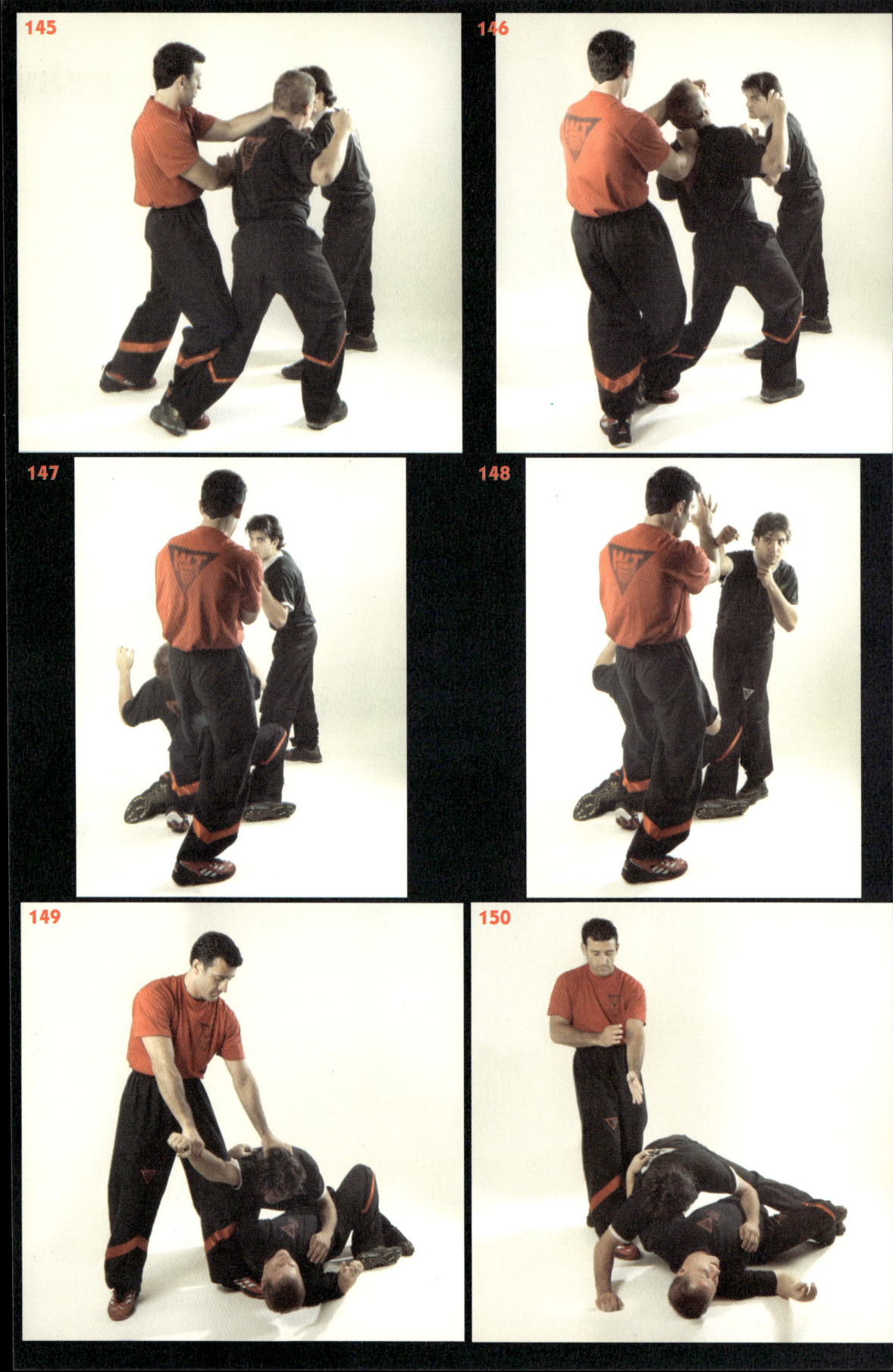

In WT, when you fight an opponent, you stay in the center of a circle while he moves in the circumference.

When you fight a group of enemies, this theory stands out for any of the opponents forming the group, but it should be amplified visualizing the whole as a great circle. You should fight the nearest opponent and, using cession and absorption techniques and performing simultaneous attacks combined with steps, you will take the opportunity to position behind him and stun him with blows at the same time. You should move in the periphery of a great circle and avoid its center, **(pictures 151 to 156).**

This way, you will be able to use him as a shield and prevail.

Move from one opponent to the other, making them getting in the way of each other. And do not forget that, as soon as you have a way out, run!

Use all your skill and attack with the most dangerous techniques, such as hit to the eyes, throat, genitals, knees, etc. Your life is at stake!

Avoid fatal errors such as:
- Placing with your back to a wall -- No chance to escape
- Positioning inside the circle.

You will be hit from different directions simultaneously
No chance to defend them all.
- Fight in the ground: No mobility at all. They will surround you and crush you. To avoid this you should master anti-grappling techniques (see Lat Sao programs below).

Seek elements which can be useful:
- Try to find a weapon: stick, iron bar, broken bottle. If you know how to use weapons this will be determinant.
- Try to position in a space limiting your opponent's movements. Take advantage of furniture, fences, cars, etc. to obstruct your enemies. We will further deal with WT Lat Sao program below, as well as its application to self-defense. Combat against several opponents is learnt in the 10th student grade (see Lat Sao programs below).

132 **The Tao of the action**

151

152

153

154

155

156

CHAPTER III
Self-Defense against armed people

This is another martial arts myth. It is, let's say, "funny", that some masters undoubtedly state that it is impossible to fight against two or more opponents -actually, it is impossible to do it using their combat system- nonetheless they have no reservations in teaching self-defense techniques against knifes or guns even.

A piece of advise: If you want to remotely have a chance to defend yourself against an armed aggressor, you must learn to fight using weapons. In WT, the student is taught to handle a knife in the 12th and last student grade. This Lat Sao program is divided into three sections:
- Knife to knife combat.
- Knife to empty-hand combat
- Empty-hand to knife combat, **(pictures 157 a 162)**.

The aim of this training is that the student knows the reality of handling a knife, so he acquires the respect due to this weapon. If your opponent has a knife and he is an expert with it, you will have no chance of surviving confronting him unarmed. Many people pretend a knife is a weapon against which you can apply disarms and other empty-hand techniques. In this Lat Sao program, the student falls from the fantasy world with some bitterness. He discovers that reality is different from films.

Again, an knife expert cannot be defeated without using weapons. The student can verify this when practicing this program. Then, what is the use of learning weapon handling? It is very important for different reasons:

Learning how to identify if your opponent knows how to use a knife. Most frequently, he will not be very skillful with this weapon. In this case, if you trained seriously, you would be able to recognize his mistakes regarding position and angles, and then apply the right strategy. But do not be overconfident, even in the hands of a fool, a sharp knife is very dangerous.

In this case, you should take advantage of your knowledge of the zones most vulnerable to cuts and protect them --neck, thoracic cavity, inner side of the arm. In these zones just the slightest cut can cause serious bleeding. You should protect them with an appropriate

134 The Tao of the action

157

158

159

160

161

162

guard. Secondly, do not try to disarm your aggressor but mainly to hit him in vital zones, especially the eyes. Thirdly, use your knowledge of the attack movements and angles in knife fighting to position yourself correctly and cancel them out. You would need an excellent judgment of timing and distance. In WT, two weapons are studied --long stick and butterfly knives. But this is at the end of the learning path. This is the reason why, **(pictures 163, 166).** in the EWTO, this art is learned in parallel with the Philippine Escrima system of master Rene Latosa. This way, you learn to handle all kinds of weapons from the beginning, thus increasing your ability to defend yourself in case you are attacked with a stick, baseball bat, knife, etc. Studying Escrima is not compulsory for WT students, but we strongly recommend it for its multiple advantages. Through the strengthening of arms and legs in Escrima, empty-hand long-distance combat greatly improves.

Escrima confers the ability to defend oneself using any kind of weapon or object:

- Pen.
- Handbag.
- Scarf.
- Stick.
- Knife.
- Broken bottle.
- Briefcase.
- Spanner.
- Hammer.
- Axe,
- keys, etc. **(see pictures 167 to 169).**

This way, your chances to overcome an attack with a knife or other weapon greatly improve.

ESCRIMA teaches you the psychomotive principles required for handling any weapon.

- Short, medium and long sticks.
- Two sticks at the same time.
- Knife.
- Two knives.

136　The Tao of the action

- Stick and knife.
- Tonfa.
- Swords: single and double.
- Spear.
- Sword and knife.
- Sword and shield.
- Machete: single and double.
- Axe: single and double.
- Palm-stick, Yawara, Vajra, Dorje.

Once again: in order to be able to defend yourself against armed aggressors, you must learn weapon fighting, **(pictures 182 to 184).**

In WT student programs 11 and 12 you deal with:
- Empty-hand defense against attack with a stick.
- The three aforementioned knife combat modes.
- Defense against firearms.

Regarding this latter point, I am afraid it is necessary again to break Hollywood and Hong Kong myths: You cannot fight against a gun. With a firearm, your enemy can kill you from several yards before you even get close to him. But sometimes, however remote, there is a chance to go unscathed, and a self-defense system must prepare the student for even the most improbable cases of success. There is only one chance to be lucky if the opponent is as silly as to get close to you with his gun. Under these circumstances, you need to concentrate at maximum in being alert and attentive in order to detect any lapse of attention or mind gap of your opponent and take advantage of it to apply a quick movement getting you out of the firing line and hitting him at the same time. Heretofore, the author tried to show some concepts related to self-defense. Now we are going to deal with how self-defense is found in our system:

WT is structured the following way
A BASIC TRAINING
A.1 Empty-hand forms:
- SIU NIM TAO (SAM PAI FUT).
- CHAM KIU TAO.
- BIU TZI TAO.

In WT, forms have different functions:
- Psychomotor education: Learning to relax and stretch your muscles and moving joints in the correct angles, etc.
- SNT also allows to cultivate internal energy and improve your health.
- Strengthening tendons and ligaments.
- Joints suppleness.
- Coordination.
- Mental concentration.

WT forms are not imaginary combats, but all their techniques are applied later, whether in Chi Sao, Chi Gerk or Lat Sao.

A.2 Steps:
Displacement training.

A.3 Complementary exercises.
- Hitting the triple bag with arms and legs.

- Many other: (specific stretching, strength and coordination exercises).

B. Sensitiveness training.
   Chi Sao:
   - Dan Chi Sao (one hand).
   - Poon Sao (rolling both hands).
   - Chi Sao sections.
   - Free Chi Sao (Chi Sao combat).

   Chi Gerk: Sticky legs.

C. Lat Sao: Application to combat and self-defense.
   - Semi-free Lat Sao exercises.
   - Free combat with protectors.

D. Wooden dummy training.

E. Weapons.
   - Long stick.
   - Butterfly knives.

In the following pages Lat Sao program of the 12 student grades is explained. Through them, all WT concepts applied to self-defense are trained.

140 **The Tao of the action**

Sifu Javier Gutiérrez

CHAPTER IV
The secrets of combat effectiveness

LAT-SAO: Free-fight pedagogy. In the course of learning any martial art, three stages can be defined:

1. Learning how to move your body. Individual training of basic techniques. Development of basic body mechanics.

2. Applying techniques through preset exercised with a partner. Development of elementary distance sense.

3. Free fight. Techniques are freely applied reacting in a spontaneous and unconscious way.

Frequently, however successfully completing the first two stages does not result in the achievement of equally valid skills in free fight, the third and last stage of training, which in fact gives sense to the whole thing. Actually, free-fight is a situation completely different from the first two stages. The main difference cannot be found in body mechanics, as movements present no additional difficulty, but in the need of intelligently react to unforeseeable problems (actions of your opponent). This response must unavoidably come from the unconscious, as the speed of movements prevents any reflection to choose a technique. Doubt, fear and Doubt, fear and stiffness will block spontaneous reactions. Conversely, sensitiveness, relaxation and flexibility favor effectiveness. In WingTsun, this problem has been overcome through sensitiveness exercises which develop unconscious reactions to the opponent's actions -- Chi Sao (sticky hands) and Chi Gerk (sticky legs). However, this is a only a partial solution, as it starts in a situation of contact of both partners' arms and/or legs. Traditionally, after completing this stage, free combat was practiced, as learning was mainly private and Sifu could lead the student through increasing difficulty levels until achieving full realism. When learning became more crowded, this method was rendered useless, thus creating a gap between Chi Sao and free fight which the student had to fulfill by himself. Many did not or spent too much time to succeed. Keith R. Kernspecht, Great WT Master, with the aim of overcoming this problem, set up a learning method acting as a transition between the first two stages (basic techniques and Chi Sao) and free fight. So, Lat Sao programs were born, following the existing student grades division created by his Sifu, Great Master Leung Ting. Each student grade was comprised of different techniques, exercises, forms and Chi Sao

which the student had to work and develop in before passing to the next. Now a specific Lat Sao program is added in each grade. This method was devised under very precise guidelines:
- The method must be lively, i.e., to have surprise factor and spontaneity.
- The method must create unexpected situations corresponding to any kind of actions belonging to other styles, such as hits, sweepings, kicks, take-downs, throws (Boxing, Wrestling, Kickboxing, Kung Fu, etc.). Each WingTsun man should effectively apply his own style when confronted to these actions. So, in training, one of the students would act as "the bad guy", attacking using any kind of non-WingTsun techniques for a wide range of self-defense situations. His/her partner would play the "good guy" role of WT fighter, neutralizing their actions through WT techniques. This way, the vicious circle of training WT to fight against WT is broken. The real situation of self-defense is "WT against what may come". Roles would be freely exchanged, thus guaranteeing the surprise factor.
- The method must lead the student to understand the application of movements learnt in forms and Chi Sao in combat and the underlying principles.
- The method must be safe, with no accident risk, and available to anyone. It should not be necessary to apply full contact to be effective.
- The method must be flexible, enabling each teacher to introduce new elements according to his/her creativity.
- The method must be progressive and edifying for the student each time he/she achieves a new skill level. So, perception and execution of the first student grade program by a beginner and an advanced student is very different.
- The method must be effective. It really must deliver adaptability, relaxation, flexibility and spontaneity in unexpected conditions. Follows an explanation of the first Lat Sao programs corresponding to the first student grades (from the beginning to more or less two years of practice).

Program 1

This program is totally basic. Long distance or "transition" (pre-contact) distance is trained.

1. Universal solution

Your opponent is away from you and he attacks. First, attacks should be slow and simple (kicks, punches). Then, actions are sped up and feints and pace changes, threats, combinations and all kinds of come-ins, hits, jerks, take-down attempts (wrestling-like), etc. are introduced. WingTsun student counterattacks applying the first principle (advance towards your enemy, staying covered and, if the way is clear hit continuously), using the movement called "Universal solution" regardless the attack of his opponent. To succeed, WingTsun student must develop a precise assessment of distance to unconsciously react and advance as soon as his enemy enters the "critical zone". The exercise allows removing instinctive unintelligent reactions, like going back, doubting or letting yourself being fooled by feints.

2. Long contact situation

Enlarging distance to attack low kicks and then shorten it back. Both partners launch straight punches through the central line. Contact is made in the wrist area **(pictures 170, 171).** Their right feet are contacting each other. Punches are continuous and, if both do their job properly, punches neutralize each other. Any force in excess or deviation from the central line must be taken advantage of through any of the four basic reactions. These reactions allow to give way and guide your opponent's arm (reactions are Tan, Bong, Cham and Kao) while you launch a simultaneous counterattack using the other arm (applying the non-resistance principle). One arm sticks to the opponent's until replaced by the other arm. If your arm is taken back before the other arm hit reaches your opponent, a gap will be created which your partner will probably use unconsciously by throwing a punch immediately (applying sensitiveness and following the principle of "if your enemy leaves a gap, hit through it"). This time, both partners act as WT fighters, moving simultaneously. From time to time, one of them unexpectedly

144 **The Tao of the action**

makes a sudden movement trying to break down the other's guard. The disconcert so created is used to gain distance and kick (adopting the role of "other style man"), **(pictures 172, 173).**

172

173

WT man should avoid to be taken by surprise and, if possible, to take advantage of the gap created by his opponent when separating, by launching a WT kick immediately. If this kick does not reach him, defend his kick using Yap Gerk, etc. and immediately close the distance again with an attack by any of them. The separation range (distance opening) ranges from very long to very short, thus making the student to learn to recognize distances. Kicks can be headed to any height, but special attention is paid to low kicks (aimed to testicles and legs) as they are the most difficult to defend. This can be combined with high hits to train the WT man keeping the arm guard high. This comings and goings are freely performed starting in the punch exchange long contact situation.

3. Anti-ground fighting exercises

Ya hemos hablado antes de los intentos de derribo. Otra parte es el trabajo en el que uno está en el suelo boca arriba y adopta la guardia de WT y el otro está separado intentando apartar el pie. (Ver el siguiente capítulo).

Take-down attempts have been dealt with above. Other part of this work is made with one of the students is lying on the floor, face up, with WT guard. The other is away from him, trying to put his foot away (see next chapter).

Program 2

Incluye todo lo hecho en el primero pero ahora por los dos lados It comprises the whole first program work but using both left and right sides. A new element is introduced -passing from straight punches exchange in long contact to sharply close distance with a strong slap on your advanced arm. The objective of this slap is to disconcert and throw off balance the WT man and punch him in the trunk simultaneously, then getting out with a low kick. The student playing the role of WT man **(pictures 174, 176)** will then have to react properly. Roles will be exchanged without warning.

Program 3

This is one of the most difficult programs, as Chi Sao learning is started (Darn Chi Sao in fact; one-hand Chi Sao, which belongs to the third student program or grade). Starting in the long contact situation, one of the students gets in with a punch crossing the central line. His partner gives way to this punch with Bong Sao, turn and simultaneous counterattack **(picture 177)**. The first, in turn, defends and the defender (now attacker) grips his arm and pulls it with Lap Sao and Kwa Choy **(picture 178)**. The first follows the pull with a simultaneous step, Tan Sao and punch. The second goes on with Pak Sao-punch. The four reactions are trained here, as well as neutralizing grips, all without warning, trying to surprise and unbalance. Anti-ground fighting exercises are closer, getting to neck and legs.

Program 4

It goes more deeply in the mid distance, learning how to turn and follow your opponent's movements, as well as to apply simultaneous attack and defense. Anti-ground fighting exercises include hitting while being taken to the floor. Also, when lying face up, you learn to trap your opponent when he has passed the first leg barrier applying Gerk and other knee reactions.

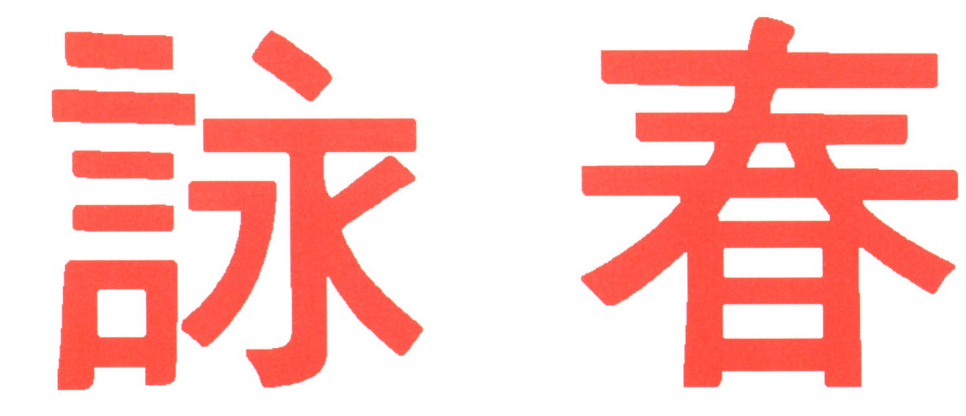

詠 春

Program 5

Short distance -- knees, elbows and body-to-body. Here, starting from the long contact situation, your partner tries to pass your guard in order to grab your head. You apply a flexible reaction to provide no support to his attack and thus cancel it out. Once he grabbed your head, your partner pulls it downwards while hitting your trunk or head using knees and elbows **(pictures 184 to 187).** You, in turn, neutralize these hits by controlling his arms with your hands and his knee-blows with your elbows. When you detect a lack of energy, counterattack (Chi Sao application). Your partner will try to throw you off balance by pulls, trips, etc. Elbows against elbows -- from the long contact position, your partner closes the distance by controlling your arm and getting in elbowing, following the movement which can be found de la 2nd form (Chamkiu Tao), **(pictures 179, 183).** You learn to give way in short distance, create gaps and elbow through those gaps, counterattacking his attempts. According to pressure, there are different reaction possibilities for which sensitiveness is required. Anti-ground fighting exercises: body-to-body distance on the ground.

179

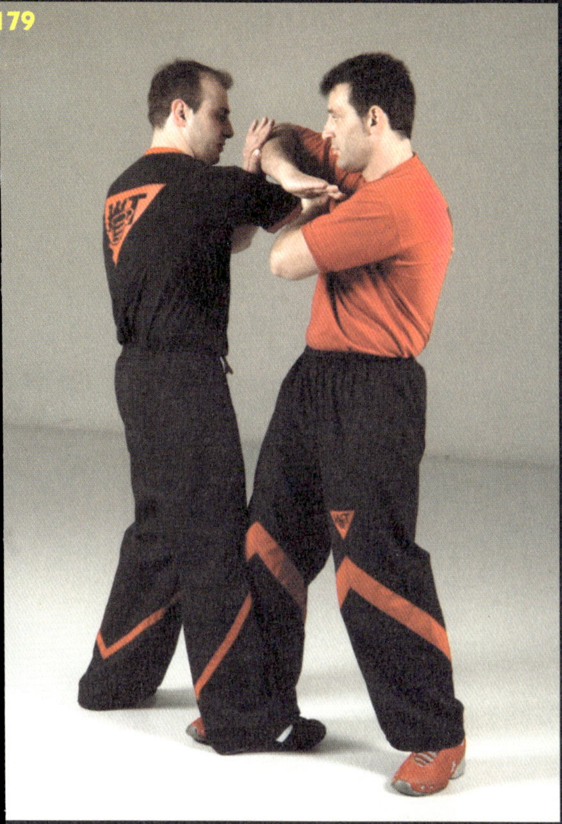

180

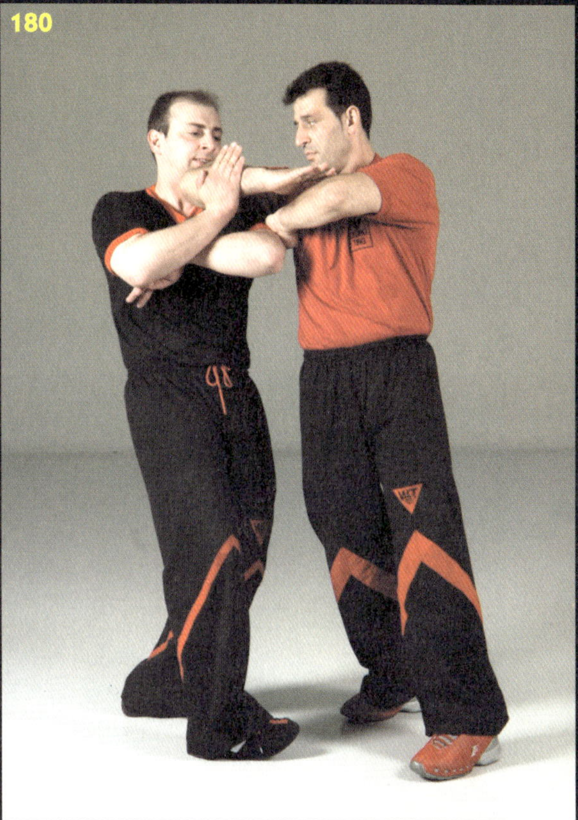

181

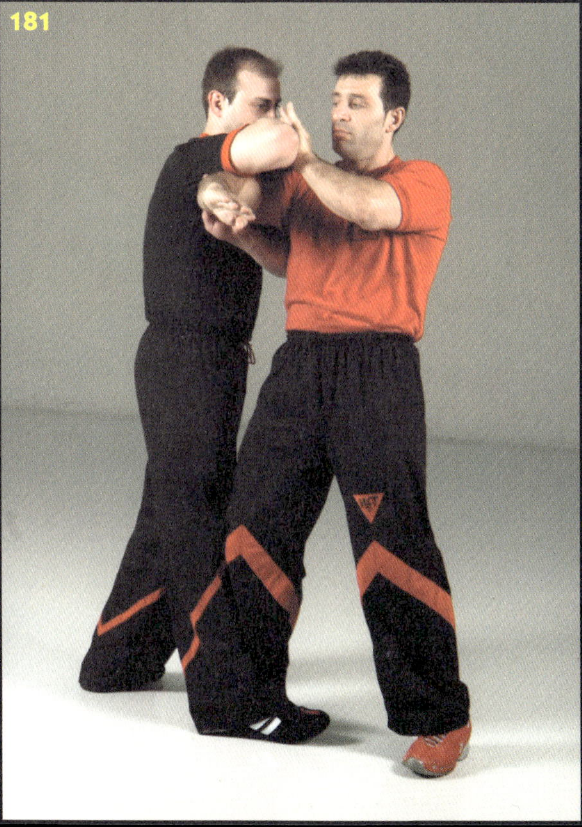

152 The Tao of the action

Following student programs (up to twelve)

You go deeper in two-arms Chi Sao, you start elementary Chi Gerk and the acquired reactions are applied in Lat Sao programs. From the eighth program, all learned skills are trained freely.

In the following programs you learn Lat Sao against several (usually three) unarmed opponents and against an armed enemy. This way, all aspects of self-defense are covered. All this can be achieved without the students getting into a scrap in free fights to contact; the method does not require this to be effective. Intensity and roughness of exercises can be easily regulated, from slow and smooth to strong and explosive, according to the progression of the student. This way, accident risk is reduced. Once the student is advanced enough and has matured all Lat Sao programs, he/she can train to full-contact with helmet and pad, or more freely but controlling blows to head and neck.

CHAPTER V
Anti-grappling

In 1990s, body-to-body combat systems were revalued (Jiu-Jitsu, wrestling, sambo, etc.) as a consequence of the emergence in the USA of "almost" no-rules fighting tournaments.

Astonished WT people saw how subjects on which they had been working on for a long time were treated as the latest novelty. There is my Sifu's book (former wrestler, nicknamed "the Strangler") where long before he had signaled the superiority of wrestlers over boxers. In 1986, Great Master Leung Ting gave a seminar where the subject of how to defend against grappling techniques was dealt with. In his book Dynamic Wing Tsun there is a picture of this seminar on which I am acting as his assistant demonstrating the "universal solution" lying on the floor. (Dynamic Wing Tsun). This is cited in order to prove that we were working on this kind of subjects long before.

This section deals with applying WT principles in the fourth (body-to-body) and fifth (ground) distance. Our aim is to clarify some ideas and correct misunderstood opinions about our style. Short-distance or anti-ground fighting techniques in our system are proprietary of our school; are not the result of adding or incorporating things from other styles.

These techniques come from the four forms of our style (Siu Nim Tao, Chum Kiu, Biu Tzi and Wooden Dummy form) and they follow exactly the same concepts as long-distance techniques. This concept can be expressed in one single word -- "adaptability" and it is applied following four tactical principles

Tactical Principles:
1. Go towards your enemy, covering yourself and, if the way is clear, hit continuously until knocking him out.
2. If you find an obstacle or the way is not clear, get rid of your own strength (relax), do not resist his force but give way to it, direct it, take advantage of this force and add yours against him.
3. Keep stuck to your opponent. If he comes, go with him; if he goes back, follow him.
4. When you find a gap in his force, hit immediately.

The practice of WT must also follow several guidelines.

1. Economy of movement. Always try to find the shortest path; the simplest movement.

2. Simultaneous attack and defense. The same movement defends you from your enemy's attack while you hit him too.

3. No preset movement. WT fighter should not follow any idea or pattern fixed beforehand. Combat develops spontaneously, and you automatically adapt to your opponent.

4. The opponent determines the movements. He unconsciously establishes reactions that you are able to perform thanks to the sensitiveness previously acquired in training. The opponent digs his own grave.

5. Continuous flow. Strictly speaking, in Leung Ting System there are not "techniques", but principles of reaction to forces applied by the opponent. Although for beginners there are names and "techniques", in expert levels these aids disappear. A movement like "Bong Sau" (lever-arm) is turned into an elbow-blow, and this into a hand-blow, which in turn transforms itself in something different. This is a flow of continuous movement where no techniques can be delimited.

The so-called "anti-ground fighting" techniques are nothing but the application of these concepts to short distances. It is always the same, in a different body position (lying down, on your knees, body-to-body). To successfully perform these techniques, WT student should have acquired certain qualities through specific training:

- The right displacements (WT steps).
- Relaxation. The ability to have a flexible force not leaving a point where the opponent could find support.
- Spring strength. The ability to absorb, to "eat" the force of your opponent and direct it to the ground. At the same time, take force from the support of your feet on the ground to the arm or leg, like a spring. The ability to generate force in the shortest movements.
- Sensitiveness to recognize your opponent's movements and to take advantage of his strength.

All those qualities are developed through specific exercise groups (Chi Sao Sections) organized by Great Master Maestro Leung Ting from his learning from G. M. Yip Man. Before that, they were taught in a private and spontaneous fashion, without a progressing structure.

Those techniques are called "anti-ground fighting" because they try to neutralize any attempt of take-down, throw, dislocation or control.

WT expert will not choose to fight in the ground as, in a self-defense situation, being back to the ground is a disadvantage; maybe the enemy is armed, or maybe other aggressors can support him. Additionally, it is very easy to get harmed fighting on the blacktop -- it is not a soft tatami mat. So, it is pretty obvious that fighting in the ground is an inadequate self-defense technique. Apart from that, if you are fighting against Wrestling or Judo experts, it is clear that you will have no option if you use techniques which they master... you will be defeated.

WT expert will not seek to choke or dislocate the opponent's members, but to control his movements using sensitiveness and hitting continuously through the gaps created, just like in other distances.

Steps

WT steps system is very different from other styles'. WT steps are learned in the wooden dummy form, so they were one of the most secret techniques of this style. G. M. Yip Man only taught the wooden dummy form to a few students, namely his sons, Sifu Leung Ting and three or four other students. Hence, it can be inferred that WT displacements are not widely known.

The first master in removing this progression order, thus revolutionizing WT was G. M. Leung Ting, who designed step exercises for beginners taken directly from the wooden dummy form.

Those steps enable you to keep your vital space and move; to control your opponent's legs; to neutralize any attempt of sweeping, grappling or take-down; and to launch kicks, knee-blows or stamps without any preparatory movement in advance. They also help to keep your genital area protected.

Anti-ground fighting techniques

Traditionally, those techniques were trained only once wooden dummy and Chi Gerk (sticky legs) techniques had been completed. That is to say, as the culmination of the empty-hand system. This learning was not structured, as in that level the student could react spontaneously and effectively, having developed the required qualities. Simply, short-distance combat situations were created and the students reacted naturally.

Nowadays, a beginners program has been established in the first five student grades. This is an introductory program, as the student lacks the sensitiveness, relaxation, stability and other qualities required to perform at 100%. However, the student gets some self-defense abilities against body-to-body techniques which make him confident under those circumstances.

Progression of the program

Neutralizing take-down or grappling attempts from the beginning. The enemy tries to get close to you in order to grapple, take down or throw you, so you cut off this attempt using steps and blows, **(pictures 188, 189).**

• The opponent manages to overcome this first barrier and starts grappling, so techniques breaking the grappling attempt while hitting at the same time should be applied, **(pictures 190 to 202).**

Sifu Víctor Gutiérrez *159*

193

194

195

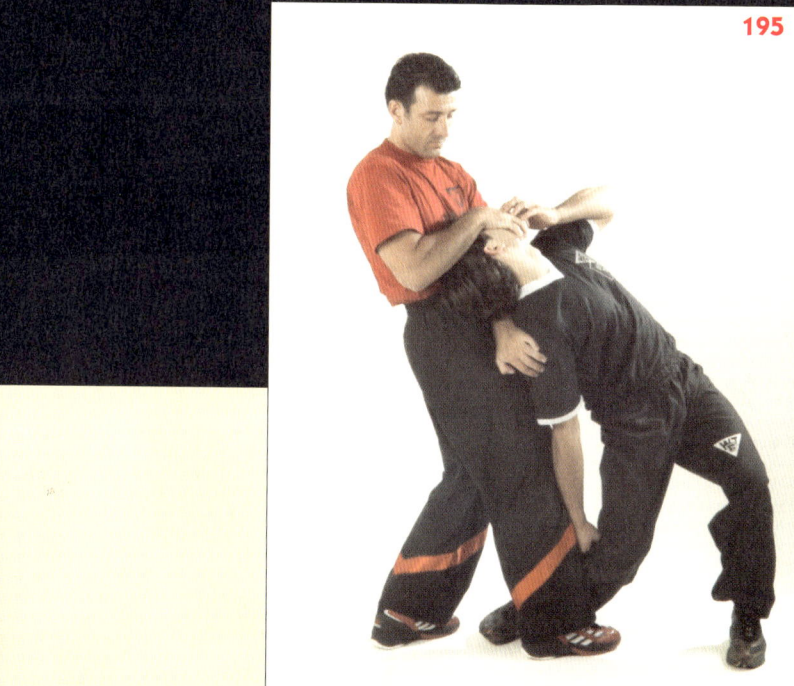

160 The Tao of the action

196

197

198

Sifu Víctor Gutiérrez 161

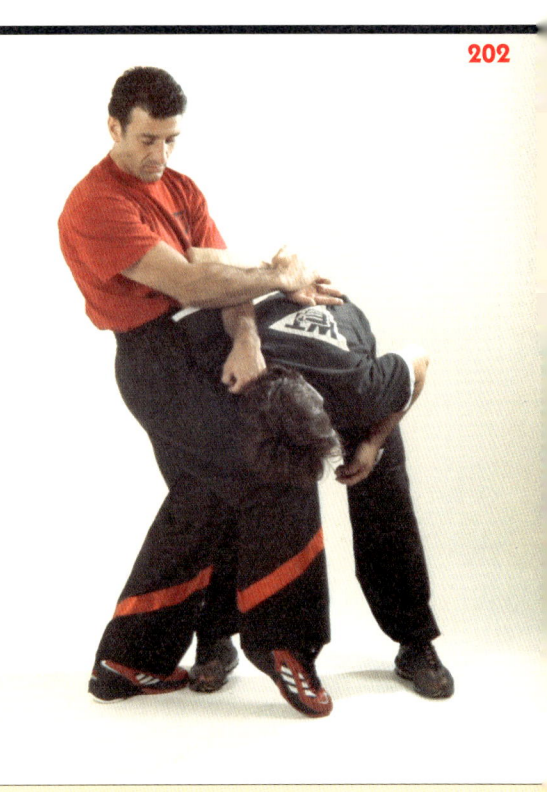

• If your WT level is low and the enemy gets to make you lose your balance and take you down, you control your fall and hit him, **(pictures 203 to 208).**

Sifu Víctor Gutiérrez 163

206

207

208

164 *The Tao of the action*

• Once in the floor, a typical WT guard (similar to the standing-up guard) is adopted and the enemy is still standing. We have three possibilities: **(pictures 209 to 216).**

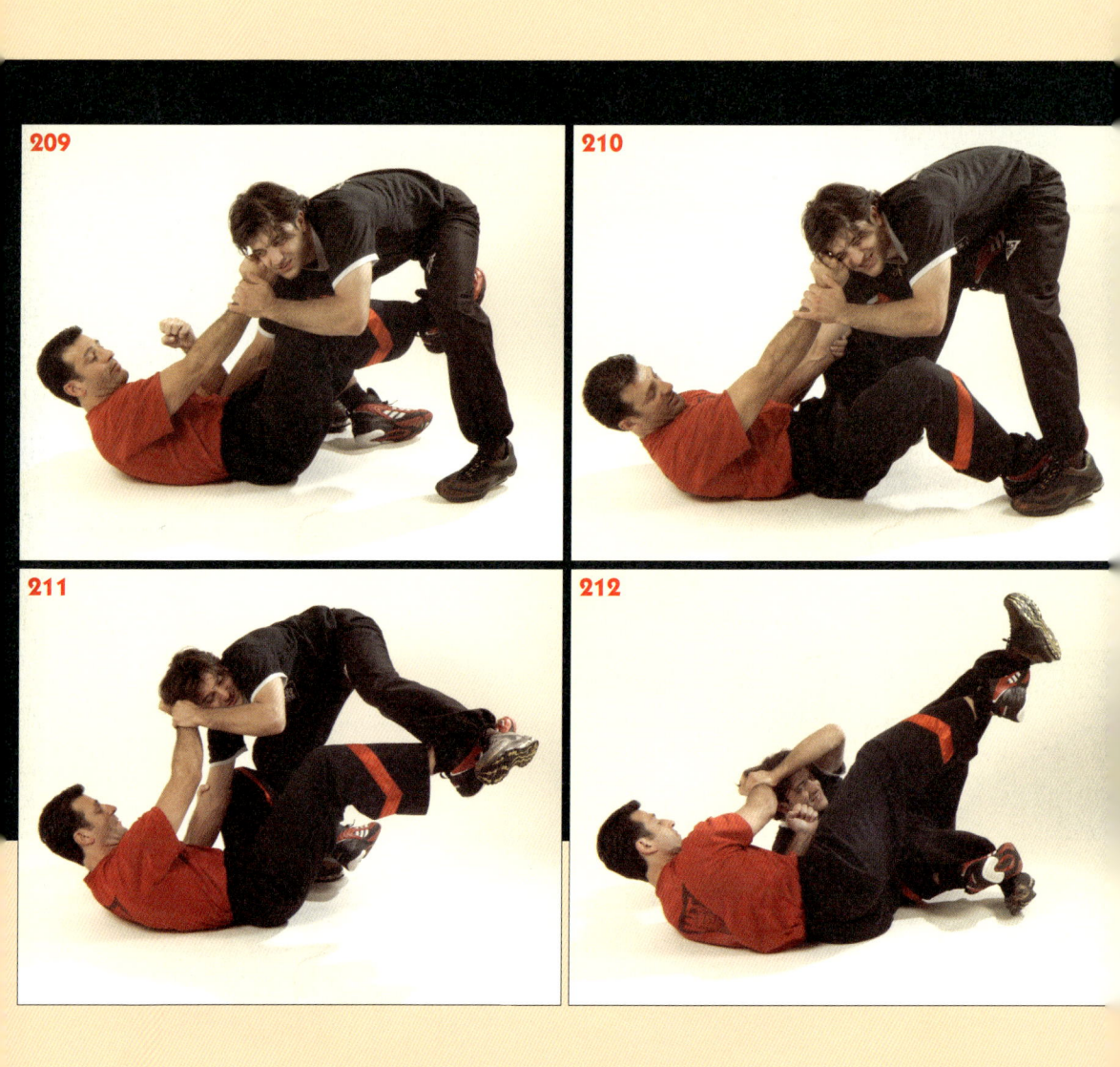

Sifu Víctor Gutiérrez 165

1. The opponent tries to put off or hold your foot to get into your guard, which you avoid using foot movements similar to SNT's Huen Sao and kicks.

2. The opponent manages to put one leg off and get in a little bit more.

3. The opponent gets a little bit closer and you control him using your knees, perfuming leg movements which enable you to take advantage of his strength, similar to Bong Sau, Tan Sau, etc. in hands.

Both adversaries on the ground, in body-to-body situation. Chances are several:

a. He is on top of you astride; you apply Chi Sao, just as if you were on your feet.

b. You are on top of him astride or laterally, using typical WT adduction stance.

c. Both are on equal basis, sideways or rolling. Techniques aimed to avoid dislocations and take advantage of force-gaps should be applied.

Potential mistakes to avoid

Trying to hold, squat, etc. That is just what a grappler wants, so it must be avoided.

The last points above are established for a case in which you stumble and fall, you slip or your opponent attacks from behind or takes you by surprise and makes you fall. WT expert, applying Taoist principles of non-resistance, is immune to take-down or dislocation attempts by experts in Wrestling, Jiu-Jitsu, Judo, etc. as proved in hundreds of occasions.

Obviously, this implies to really train those principles. That is to say, put yourself in situations like those described above with increasing difficulty. If you do not train these techniques, they do not work. So clear, so simple.

Chi Gerk

Sticky legs are the last and more advanced techniques of WT. They are learned after the applications of Wooden Dummy form. They require the highest skills and maximum usage of the "force absorption through muscle springs" principle. As "muscle springs" as wide as scapular waist and backbone are not available, difficulty is much higher. The opponent's energy must be absorbed using exclusively legs and hips, while balance is maintained using just one leg.

Chi Gerk techniques makes possible for the WT expert to softly absorb any kind of low kicks and sweepings. Through these exercises, it can be learned how to give way and attack with kicks and sweepings, trapping your opponent's legs and destroying his knees and ankles by dislocations and stamps made with your own legs. Although difficult to learn, Chi Gerk provides to the expert who manages to master it, full control over his enemy, so making him very dangerous because his attacks cause important injury.

Defense of kick

Grip and kick breaking knee and ankle.

Pictures 219, 220: Control and up-down unbalance, followed by knee.

Chi Gerk exercise.

Sifu Víctor Gutiérrez

Sifu Javier Gutiérrez

4th Part
WT and Society

CHAPTER I
The Nun Ng Mui legend and an analysis of WT's technical features

It is well-known that creation of WT is attributed to Buddhist nun NG MUI. There are no historical evidences for or against this belief, so many people doubt on the truthfulness of this story.

According to the legend, NG MUI was a master in Shaolin South Temple at Fukien. NG MUI was a Kung Fu great master and she also was advanced in years. It is said that she was already an elderly woman when Manchurians, helped by traitor monks, destroyed the temple and NG MUI had to escape.

NG MUI designed a new combat system aimed to defeat the traitor monks, who were also Shaolin Kung Fu experts. She taught this new system to Yin Wing Tsun, so the style is named after her (Wing Tsun - "Praise to the Beautiful Spring"). What can we take of this story? See some of the WT features:
- Short steps. Short movements. High positions.
- Attack in continuous burst.
- Applying principles of cession by means of developing sensitiveness.
- Economy of movement.
- Simultaneous attack and defense.

What does this have to do with NG MUI?
- NG MUI was a woman, so she was physically less strong and burly than her opponents.

She was a very old person, with the associated disadvantages (less strength and speed).

She was weaker, so she had to cultivate methods to take advantage of her opponents strength. In order to do that, she had to develop sensitiveness through Chi Sao and Chi Gerk.

Additionally, instead of entrusting effectiveness to a single blow, an avalanche of hits is preferred.

The following points are more related to the advanced years of NG MUI, which lead her to seek MAXIMUM ECONOMY OF MOVEMENT, MAXIMUM EFFECTIVENESS WITH MINIMUM EFFORT.

WT steps are really short (actually the stance is short -- the starting step is usually more than one meter long, as both feet are moved).

The strategy to fight one single opponent is to place yourself in the center of an imaginary circle, the enemy being in the periphery. Our shoulders and his shoulders are always opposite, so the stance is frontal: If the opponent wants to attack you from one side, he would need several steps, while you would only turn your full body slightly. This means that our movement will be much shorter, hence much quicker. As soon as the enemy enters the critical distance you must go to him using universal solution. WT will never use steps for feinting or going in and out. Its aim is to go through the enemy and stick to him.

Movements following the shortest route are seek. You should always try to close distance to gain maximum control over the situation.

This shows that WT is the ideal style to keep on progressing in old age. In fact, it seems to be "designed" for this purpose.

Apart from that, women tend to close legs when they are standing-up. WT has adduction, high and narrow stances... What a coincidence!

It can be concluded that WT, regardless historical truth which probably will never be known, is a "feminine design" system, which makes it very appropriate for not-so-strong people and older people too.

Sifu Víctor Gutiérrez 173

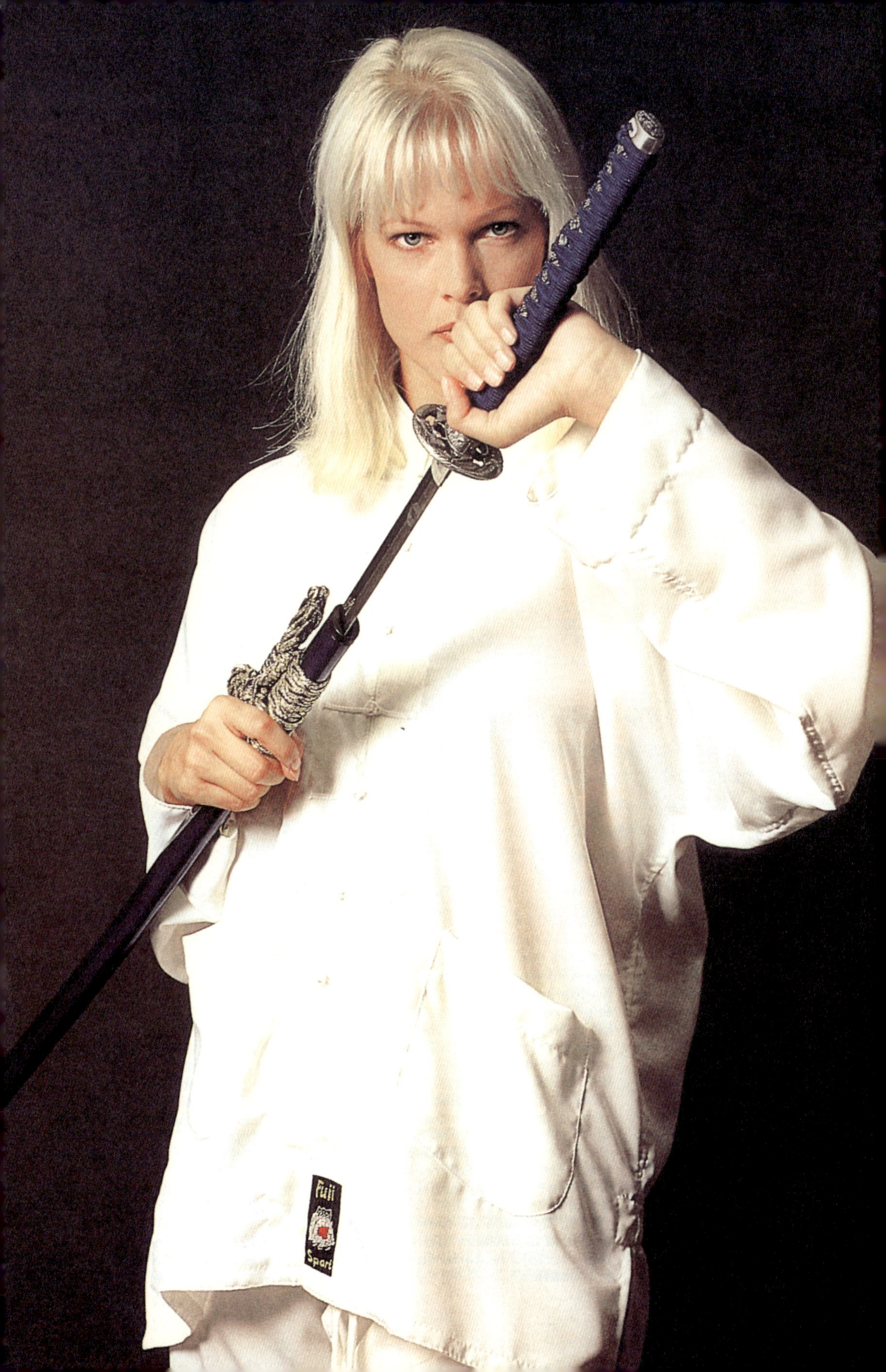
Fuji
Sport

Women and Martial Arts

CHAPTER II
A Mismatch tale

Any amateur or professional of martial arts probably realized that most of people practicing these arts belong to masculine sex. Going back in history, we see this has been always the main trend. However, one could wonder why, in the women's liberation era, this situation remains unchanged in the same extent other fields have.

Famous she-fighters

This fact cannot be attributed to a "morphological inability" of feminine sex for fighting arts as, although exceptional, there are various cases in martial arts history which prove this is not true.

In Wing Tsun lineage we find three women, which is very meaningful as, until Great Master Yip Man opened his school, there had been only a few WT-learned people.

The first is NG MUI, Buddhist nun and legendary creator of he style. Pursued by the Manchu government, several combats against other experts and fighters are attributed to her, where he succeed despite being a woman of advanced years.

Her inheritor student is famous, not just for providing such a beautiful name to the style, but for having defeated in seconds a local thug frightening the whole region for his strength and liking to fight.

Her husband, Leung Bok Chau, practiced KUNG -FU and ignored his wife's abilities.

Only after a series of coincidences he could confirm that she was able to easily defeat him. Then, he became her student. It is remarkable that Yim Wing Tsun only taught her art to her husband, who eventually transferred it to Leung Lan Kwai. Probably, for the rest of her neighbors, she was just a mere housewife like any other.

The third important woman in this destiny was the daughter-in-law of Chan Wah Sun, Great Master Yip Man's Sifu. It appears that Chan Wah Sun had an undisciplined character to his father's eye. So, Chan Wah Sun decided to tech him a lesson transferring the style's advanced techniques to his daughter-in-law instead of his son. So, Chan Yu Min had to acknowledge that his wife was at a higher Wing Tsun level than him, so having to learn from her what his father did not teach him. A great humbleness lesson.

There are other Kung-Fu styles whose creation is attributed to women, usually Buddhist nuns. The "crane seeking for food" style was developed by Buddhist nuns. Presently, the only surviving master of this style lives in Taiwan. It is also a short-boxing style, in some way similar to Wing Tsun; high and short stances, vertical punches, arm-locks, etc.

Chu Ka Shaolin style is a classic Shaolin South system. The last existing master of this style lives in Malaysia. The late martial arts history expert Don F. Draegeger made this master's name in one of his works. He met him in a research trip to South-Eastern Asia. This style is also said to have been designed by one or several Buddhist nuns.

Outside China there have been warrior women too. The late Escrima - Arnis - Kali master Floro Villabrille, a legend of Philippine martial arts, stated that the most skillful of his own masters was a woman -- Princess Josefina.

Undoubtedly, there have been more cases and there will be even more. However, the five named here are enough to confirm that women, when they take it seriously, they can be high level fighters.

Why this would not be the case at the dawn of 21st century?

Sex does matter

However, we should not celebrate or deny the obvious. There are biologic differences which cannot be obviated making women physically weaker and more vulnerable than men, you like it or not. Hormonal differences between both sexes determine that the average man is superior to the average woman in some qualities:
- STRENGTH
- WEIGHT
- HEIGHT
- AGGRESSIVENESS
- ABILITY TO PERFORM EXPLOSIVE MOVEMENTS

These qualities make the male clearly succeed in a fight. To overcome these differences, women need physical conditioning and technical training or, failing that, to use a weapon. Nature made things this way. Among qualities relevant for martial arts there is one in which women clearly overcome men: suppleness.

As regards to coordination, superficial observation may show that women are clumsier and have more problems to distinguish left and right sides of their bodies and to move them according to patterns a little bit more complicated than usual.

This "difference" actually does not depend on sex but on educational factors. Coordination varies according to the variety and familiarity with movement patterns experienced previously through your life. Males use to play various sports and games from an early age, so their nervous system is familiar with numerous positions and movement possibilities. Young girls, except in games such as rope jumping, are used to more sedentary activities so their neuromuscular system is poorer in movement patterns. Hence the clumsiness. An irrefutable evidence of how decisive is the educational factor is that gymnast and aerobic champion women display the highest level of coordination possible.

Difference between both sexes in physical terms is obvious in almost every sport. Years ago, the Dutch tried to prove the contrary. A Thai Boxing fight was arranged between a man and the prodigy Lucia Rijker, whose Muay Thai superiority over female boxers was so overwhelming that male opponents must be sought. However, they were cautious: her opponent, 11 lb lighter, was a second-class fighter, New Zealand champion but without any relevance in global rings. The result was that Lucia had to abandon the fight very quickly -- her opponent's blows were infinitely more powerful than any hit she had received from female opponents to date. Like in most sports, testosterone here still marks insuperable differences.

It is necessary to bear all this in mind to avoid being deceived by exaggeration introduced by movies: Every so often, we see C Series movies in which 100 lb model girls, looking as never having set foot in a tatami mat in her life, knock out pretended Kung Fu or Karate experts, so burly, by the way.

Of course I am not referring to real champions such as Cynthia Rothrock. Just a look to her movements makes you realize she is well trained and her blows can cause real harm. In spite of this, Cynthia would not be able to defeat a real expert in her art so easily -- most probably she would be knocked-out. But the reason for this is not just the biological difference. Part of the blame is to the use of unrealistic techniques not adapted to the feminine body. Powerful punches are not so affordable for most women, and it takes a long time to perfect them. In fact, except professional female boxers and kick-boxers, most women's punches are insufficiently offensive. It is more convenient for them to attack to more sensitive areas using more penetrating weapons; attacking to eyes or throat with hands open or semi-open; discarding hits to the trunk and seeking targets such as genitals or neck. The technique issue is dealt with below.

Why women are less interested in Martial Arts than men?

This fact should not be surprising, as that is the case in almost every sport. As a matter of fact, women are less keen on sports than men.

However, in martial arts, the contrary could be expected. Are nor women the main victims of home and street violence? Of course they are. This situation, in existence from the dawn of humanity, is based on the aforementioned biological differences, making women the easiest prey for the inevitable savage. So, any method which enable women to overcome the biological inequality and to put their fighting skills to the same level of men should be very attractive for modern women. But this is not the case.

What are the reasons for this?

1. Social prejudice

"This is not much feminine". "That is for mannish women". "This is something for thugs and louts". Statements like these can be heard even today, at the beginning of 21st century, in many homes where a girl shows desire for start practicing fighting arts. On the strength of her personality and motivation will depend that she changes her mind or not. Even greater pressure will bear those women confronting oppression from his small-minded --fearful?-- boyfriend or husband. All in all, any woman, especially over 30, practicing a martial art whatsoever is at least "exotic". And exoticism is even greater if it is a contact style.

2. Inner prejudice

Many Eastern great masters, when asked about women in their martial arts often answered things like: "It is good for women to practice this art, but they should concentrate in Katas, avoiding combat". And even Western masters thought that way! I remember a statement by a famous Karate champion and national coach, talking about women kumite competition: "I do not like to see women fighting; it is better for them to make love".

Although taken out of context, these statements reveal certain prejudice among many students and masters like "This is really a men thing; no good for women". No matter what experiences or circumstances lead to think this way, the truth is that this attitude is a hindrance for things to change.

3. Mistaken ideas

Some women hesitate to start martial arts because they mistakenly believe that those arts masculinize woman body. Nothing could be further from the truth. Physical activity improves woman figure. And martial arts are one of the most all-round sports; surely much more beneficial for woman look than soccer or athletics.

Women are masculinized by sport when take steroids (see Miss Olympia contestants) or suffer hormonal disorders. It can be added that some martial arts expert women have been offered photo sessions because of their beauty. This is the case of French kick boxing and boxing world champion Valerie Henin, living evidence that a woman can be pretty, good mother and hitting like the devil.

4. Not used to physical exercise

Some girls initially suffer from never having exercised their bodies. I can tell them that martial arts are not more demanding than aerobic or fitness and, if they persist, their body will get used to physical activity. Above all, they should train gradually, at their own pace. Following these principles, they are able to follow the class like everybody else very soon. This is not a women-specific problem. Anyone leading a sedentary life can encounter this difficulty.

5. Initial shyness

Something dramatically deferent for many women is to find themselves in a class attended exclusively by men. The "I'm the only girl" syndrome is sometimes determinant. A vicious circle is created:

"There are no girls in the class, so I'm not joining; there are still no girls because I'm not joining".

Some possible solutions for this problem are analyzed below.

6. Fear of injury

Fear does not belong to one of both sexes. Everybody is afraid of being hit, to a greater or lesser extent. In this case, fear can be greater when training with men.

An adequate pedagogy which enables a woman to progressively gain basic self-confidence before practicing combat, along with a welcoming atmosphere by training partners, is the best way to remove this hindrance.

How to change this situation?

There is not an infallible formula, but we can analyze some possible solutions to the aforementioned problems.

A. Problems 1, 2 and 3 can be corrected simply providing proper information.

B. For problems 4, 5 and 6 a method consisting in classes or seminars only for women can be used. This systems has pros and cons.

Advantages: From the beginning, shyness associated with being the only girl in a boys class is removed. Fear of being hit is reduced, as training partners have more or less the same strength. Additionally, pace and intensity of training can be better adapted.

Disadvantages: They do not train with men, so they go far off a real self-defense situation. Their techniques will not be valid, as in training they have an opponent much less strong than the one they would find in a real confrontation.

An interesting strategy would be to start with an exclusively women group until the girls reach a certain level of basic skills and sufficient physical condition. Then, they would be gradually transferred to a mixed class -- first, once a week; three months later, two or more.

C. Presenting an extensive approach to Martial Arts
1. Do not focus on sports aspects

Indeed, this is by far the least interesting aspect, not just for women but for most people. Additionally, sports deviate training from self-defense objectives, which are the base for other psychological, cultural and professional benefits.

2. Do not overlook self-defense

What distinguishes martial arts from other activities is the ability to overcome biological determinism of male physical superiority.

If we want this to be real, not another advertising ploy, training must follow a thorough process, which is explained in detail in the last part of this chapter.

3. Talking about side physical and psychological benefits

3.1 Physique: Many women perform hard aerobic sessions daily. What is their motivation to bear this? Improving their physique. The right martial arts training provides the same result, and it also offers many other advantages that aerobic could never provide. In fact, some aerobic coaches include Karate, Kung fu or Boxing techniques in their aerobic exercises because of their attractiveness. Would not be better to go straight to the source, to martial arts?

3.2 Health: Here we are not referring to the benefits any kind of physical exercise provide. Many martial arts include breathing and concentration exercises, static or moving, providing an additional health improvement.

3.3 Mind: Everyone starting martial arts seeks to increase self-confidence, to get an energy and assurance feeling. We can state with no fear of exaggeration that there is no activity which can provide such a great improvement in self-esteem and confidence as achieving a real high level in martial arts (provided that the right attitude has been maintained during learning).

Any woman going through this physical and psychological training process will immediately reject any discriminatory or degrading behavior as well as battering or abuse. She would feel responsible of her life and would not be a victim anymore. Other well known benefits are: improvement of concentration and decision-making skills and stress release.

4. Martial Arts and women's liberation

Reading through this chapter makes clear that martial arts have a lot to contribute to women's liberation and equal rights for both sexes. Tackling one of the key points of discriminatory treatment suffered by women for millenniums, that is to say, male physical superiority, martial arts help this equality of rights come true.

5. Focusing on martial arts cultural aspects

Many women feel attracted by cultural aspects of Eastern civilizations and feel disappointed about what they see as insufficient information or interest by their instructors towards these issues. Buddhism, Taoism and Confucianism form the mental and pedagogic structure of, for instance, Chinese Kung Fu. Martial arts history can be easily correlated to history and cultural display of their countries of origin, not just for the expert's eye. It is not necessary to give a lecture on the matter. Just drop an anecdote, statement or reference from time to time. And, above all, being able to provide a consistent and correct answer when asked about these issues. Nowadays, traveling to the Far East is not unusual. Some people felt awakening their interest in martial arts following a visit to China, Japan or Thailand. Proper knowledge of the roots of your style would be helpful to understand the bridge between vacation to the East and your gym's tatami.

6. Professionalization?

The number of truly martial arts qualified girls in teaching is so small. Is there a demand for martial arts female masters? No one can answer for certain, but probably more girls would allow themselves to be drawn towards martial arts if they would find female teachers. On the other hand, the best evidence of the effectiveness of a style would be a woman able to lead, with authority and physical power to support it, a class with several men.

7. Presenting feminine role models to follow

Apart from a few action film stars, it is pretty obvious that girls have not many idol women to identify with. In these days, the vast majority of the great masters coping magazine pages are men. Women usually appear in those magazines because of sports achievements, not for their specific gravity as masters or leaders of their style.

This point is the hardest to change, but the way would be to pay more attention to the existing --however scarce-- high-level female students.

Why most women do not achieve high effectiveness in combat?

1. Lack of training

It is funny to see how some women intend to achieve the same level as their male counterparts, training a half or a quarter of the time they do. Many are happy with training a couple of hours a week but, hey, they intend to quickly achieve the same self-defense skills than others. Obviously, you cannot go far this way. At least, women should train the same as men. It is common sense. And not only in quantitative but in qualitative terms.

A 135 lb short man would have to train harder if he wants to achieve the same effectiveness as a 6 ft 220 lb muscle-built man. Why? Just because he would have to use technique to make up for the lack of strength and weight. That simple. Therefore, it is not a matter of sexual discrimination.

2. Use of inadequate techniques

This point has been already dealt with. Women should preferably use techniques more determinant than the usual punch or the most common kicks. They should attack more sensitive areas such as eyes, throat, genitals or knees. Their displacements need to be much better than a man's. And they should acquire great mobility enabling her to avoid direct crash and to use penetration angles not requiring great power. They should have great skills for giving way to the force of their opponent and taking advantage of it.

If they want to display real power in the techniques performed, they should concentrate in realistic training and avoiding wasting time in display techniques and movement aesthetics. They should emphasize practicing with partners and properly assessing distance, not paying too much attention to individual forms.

3. Insufficient development of power and explosiveness

Girls, more than anybody else, should strive for technical finesse required to apply all body weight in every hit. Coordination of the various joint levers in a flowing explosive but relaxed movement must be perfected at maximum through exercises developed to this aim. In parallel with this, sufficient physical condition should be acquired. Women's joints are looser and weaker, so especially fingers, wrists, elbows, knees, ankles and hips should be strengthened.

Specifically designed weight training can be very beneficial. Fitness should not be gotten mixed up with bodybuilding or weight-lifting. Above all, legs, tendons and joints training should be emphasized.

Waist and scapular area are the power sources, in coordination with legs, so they should be addressed with specific exercises. It is a proven fact that a properly trained woman is stronger than an untrained (or less trained) man, this not implying a masculinization of her morphology. In fact, power exercises for kicks (sandbag, isokinetic push of partner, etc.) are the best for shaping women's thighs and hips. So, they not just train the crucial aspect of power but they also improve their look.

Conclusion

Experience proves that women are able to achieve a high level of skills in any martial art, but it can be easily observed that only a few succeed. To turn this situation it is necessary to forget about myths and exaggeration and use the right methodology. Combining realism and enthusiasm is the only way for martial arts to pass the equal rights course in 21st century.

Sifu Víctor Gutiérrez 187

CHAPTER III
WT, Health and Chi Kung

The Chinese people have been using Kung Fu from time immemorial as a self-defense, health and fitness method.

WT is a combat system which, in history, has been practiced mainly for self-defense. Personally, I always focused on this aspect, self-defense, not paying too much attention to other fields of WT (Taoism, Confucianism, Buddhism, Chinese culture and language, health and medicine, etc.).

However, among my students doctors, engineers, physical education teachers, acupuncturists, osteopaths, psychologists, physiotherapists, Qigong teachers, etc. can be found.

Those students helped me to appreciate other aspects of WT.

Entire pages of this book, especially those dealing with WT biomechanics and kinesiology are the product of advise provided by doctors, osteopaths and other professionals devoted to fields related to medicine.

The present chapter has been written thanks to cooperation with doctors, acupuncturists Qigong teachers, as well as my learning from my Sigung, Great Master Leung Ting and my Sifu K. R. Kernspecht.

At the moment, some of these people are undertaking research projects which may be very interesting in fields such as WT and neurology, or WT and Qigong, WT and rehabilitation, WT and psychology, or WT and education. Over the time it will be seen if these projects are translated into real experiences.

WT and functional longevity

The ability to maintain or even improve physical and mental skills over the time, even at advanced years (the so-called old age), is what I mean by functional longevity. Can any WT or other style martial artist keep on improving constantly over 40, 50 or 60 years old?

To answer this question, factors impacting functional impairment linked to age should be addressed:

- **In locomotor system:**
- **Ageing is usually linked to the following problems.**
- **Decrease in joint mobility:** Joints get stiffer. But, is ageing the

real cause? Would it be a sedentary life and lack of training? Anyone practicing movement and stretching can keep his/her suppleness for life.

• **Osteoporosis:** Bone demineralization may be prevented in two ways.

• **Diet:** The key point is not to take calcium but to avoid losing it and to improve its absorption. To this end, other elements apart from calcium have to be taken into account: magnesium, phosphor and trace elements such as fluoride, etc. Additionally, a balance between acidifying and basifying elements should exist.

• **Physical exercise:** It has been proved that muscle activity increases calcium fixation to bones, and it is the best preventive and therapeutic treatment. In WT we find movements for every joint, as well as stretching and exercises toning-up muscles. This guarantees longevity for your locomotor system.

• **Cardiovascular system:** The fearsome heart attack, hypertension, arteriosclerosis, or cholesterol, main factors affecting circulatory impairment are prevented and treated through aerobic exercise and healthy eating. WT as aerobic exercise is also helpful in this aspect.

• **Brain and nervous system:** Brain deterioration giving rise to senile dementia, loss of memory and other deficiencies is a very important issue in developed countries.

Brain gymnastics systems are being researched in order to prevent and to treat those problems. It has been observed that people keeping a high level of intellectual and/or artistic activity preserve their faculties much better. WT has a couple of interesting things to say:

• **Chi Sao is a great exercise for brain;** it works both hemispheres, cultivates ambidexterity, develops new inter-neuron links and rises proprioceptive and kinesthetic conscience.

• **The SNT** form (see below) can be practiced as a meditation form (see also chapter III of 1ª part on the meditation).

WT, like any other learning process, rises mental features such as curiosity, will and project or goal setting. Precisely these elements tend to vanish with ageing.

WT and martial longevity

Martial longevity relates to the ability to maintain or even improve fighting skills even at advanced years (60, 70 and above). Martial longevity necessarily implies functional longevity. But it also requires the right technical structure for prevailing circumstances. As explained above, in the section about nun NG MUI legend, WT was supposedly developed by an old Buddhist nun who defeated other relevant fighters. WT technical features perfectly fit with the martial longevity objective.

WT and psychology

WT can be linked to psychotherapy aimed to favor self-esteem, self-confidence, calmness and positive attitude. It could also be helpful in depression, shyness, anxiety or stress therapy.

How? In different ways:

• Practicing dynamic rooting and active force projection activates stability, firmness, calmness and confidence feelings. If combined with visualization and affirmation techniques, its effect would be multiplied.

• Depression is a condition inhibiting own force and power. A martial art such as WT is the ideal way to get connected to your own energy, especially if combined with a specific mental treatment therapy.

• WT favors socialization, as it is practiced in physical contact and cooperating with your partners' learning. Lack of physical contact can trigger mental disorders, as it is widely know.

• Other benefits:
• Concentration improvement.
• Spatial orientation improvement.
• Creativity improvement due to brain's right side stimulation.
• Body conscience improvement.
• Imagination improvement.

As we can see here, possibilities of applying WT in education (especially children education) are enormous.

WT and Chi Kung (Qigong)

Connection between WT and Chi Kung (Qigong) has been repeatedly mentioned and seldom explained.
This connection can be established in a number of points:
Chi Sao and Chi Kung (Qigong).
Some people mistakenly believe that "Chi" in Chi Kung and "Chi" in Chi Sao, are the same word. Nothing could be further from the truth.
• Chi in Chi Kung means air, breathing, vitality, vital energy.
• Chi in Chi Sao means sticky, adhesive.
Their ideograms are different.
Connection between Chi Sao and Chi Kung goes in a different course.
Chi Sao develops dynamic rooting and Chi Kung is also based in rooting.
Chi Sao cultivates interior (proprioceptive) conscience and relaxation, creating subjective connections into the body. So, different body parts consciously react with each other giving rise to a psychosomatic unit. Chi Kung aims the same goal, but there are interesting differences. Chi Kung is trained alone. Sometimes, people practicing Chi Kung do not get the desired effect because they lack references about what to feel. Chi Sao is trained with a partner, so we have a trial - error - correction method for learning (to see part II chapter III). So, Chi Sao can improve and speed up your Chi Kung practice. Chi Sao offers objective tests to really know if you are rooted or not, or if you can make energy "explode". Chi Kung is practiced individually, so you can be led to error, believing you have skills you really have not developed yet.

Siu NimTtao, forms and Chi Kung

SNT form (form or technical outline of the "little idea") is the mother form of all WT. This form has many functions:
• It is a source of "little ideas" or technical principles. So, every movement in SNT is a seed of concepts from which numerous Chi Sao and Lat Sao exercises can be drawn for application and learning. For instance, all Darn Chi Sao movements come from the third section of SNT.
• It shows relaxation and proper psychomotor activity for movement.

• It enables cultivating vital energy, so it is a Chi Kung exercise at the end of the day, although in WT we prefer not to use this term.

SNT is divided in 8 technical sections. Each time the arms return to the hips, a section is completed. Sections, as for movements, are comprised of simultaneous (arms moving together) and alternate (arms moving separately; first the left arm and then the right) sections.

Sections 1 - 4 and 8 are simultaneous. Te rest are alternate.

From the pedagogic standpoint, traditionally SNT was taught in three parts or stages, hence some people mistakenly think it has just three sections.

SNT provides any number of "little ideas" or working principles for combat and training, but it also provides numerous internal and external energy working principles. We can bundle around twelve concepts or training methods contained in SNT, through which a wide range of energy exercises can be drawn. Explaining all this in full detail would require a full thick book. Here I will confine myself to setting out a few details of the form itself.

Differences between the old form and the version of Yip Man (received of its Teacher Chan Wah San).

1. Stance is lower and wider in the original form; knees are closer to each other.

2. In the original form, the third section has just one Tan Sao, two Fuk Sao and three Wu Sao. So it was called "Sam Pai Fut" (to pray to Buddha three times), because of the three Wu Sao. When it was modified, its performance was accelerated. To make up for it, a new Fuk Sao and one Wu Sao were added. But the name "Sam Pai Fut" did not match with it anymore -- there was a Wu Sao in excess. This is the answer for this inconsistency. Movements in this third sections are the same, with slight variations in Fuk Sao, Wu Sao and when taking in the fist at the end. Some guidelines about where and how to focus imagination during Fuk Sao and when taking in the fist were also added. Movements in this third section are performed very slowly, apparently unmoving, but in a continuous movement actually. This movement is so slow that it is almost imperceptible, but it should never stop. This reaction is the longest and "vigorous" in the form.

3. The fourth section is where more changes can be found. The outline is the same, but movements are transformed. There is a work of actively stretching tendons and joints; there is a resonant breathing exercise stimulating internal organs; there is a dynamic tension exercise and some other differences, although order and movements are analogous.

The rest of the form is almost unchanged.

Breathing in both versions of the form should be the same -- abdominal, slow, deep, breathing in through the nose and breathing out through the mouth audibly. So, if the third section is performed slowly, "martial" Siu Nim Tao is useful for cultivating Chi and improving health too. As Wing Tsun enthusiasts may remember, Great Master Yip Man spent one hour to perform the Siu Nim Tao form, with the aim of strengthening his health.

4. The old form displays exactly 108 points or movements. Adding a few more movements in the martial version made it not complying with the 108 points rule.

Overview and analysis of original Siu Nim Tao benefits and advantages

This issue is addressed from three points of view: energy, physical/technical and psychological.

Energy aspects

1. Stance: Adduction stance is not used exclusively in Wing Tsun. There are static Qigong exercises consisting only of adopting a position with arms like embracing a tree. Some Qigong teachers state this stance has energetic properties such as attracting energy from the ground through the legs and backbone to the arms, or increasing energy in kidneys.

2. Abdominal breathing

Attention must be focused on umbilical and infra-umbilical regions. According to Qigong Masters and Chinese ancient medicine, it was traditionally thought that the body's main energy center is located in this area. This makes Chi to gather in this center (called lower Dan Tien and associated to kidney and sexual organs), thus increasing vitality of the whole organism and renewing it inside.

3. The "smoking body"
When this form is correctly performed, your body

gathers energy and blood circulation is intensified producing heat. If exterior temperature is mild, you will sweat profusely. Otherwise, if environment is cold, sweat will be released as vapor, thus giving the impression of smoking body.

4. The "black palm"

In a higher level, when performing third section Tan Sao slowly, blood flow is intensified in the palm of your hand and could even get so hot that it turns purple. When changing your arm position by turning your wrist (Huen Sao), passing to Wu Sao position, your palm will suddenly its natural color, as if by magic. There are legends about the mortal hit of this Shi-loaded "black palm". Sifu Leung Ting usually gives demonstrations in which, after getting this effect, he hits people without any special consequence. According to him, this is another Kung Fu myth. So, Siu Nim Tao can be considered a Qigong exercise providing health and energy.

Physical-technical aspects

1. Adduction stance is very useful for legs. It improves ground rooting capabilities, displacements and kicking power.
2. Third section arm movements (Tan Sau, Wu Sao, Huen Sao, Fuk Sao) are performed extremely slow, as explained above. Strength driving the arm slowly must come from elbow, while wrist and biceps muscles are relaxed. This form of exercising develops body conscience of muscles, joints and their movements, making it more and more fine and precise, learning to relax antagonist muscles, thus increasing movement power and speed. This work is complemented by one of the fourth section exercises, consisting of active stretching of muscles, tendons, ligaments and fascia, thus lengthening your arm several centimeters (it is worth seeing Great Master Leung Ting performing this exercise). If sections 3 and 4 are analyzed from the biomechanics standpoint, we can understand how they can help to improve our technique.

Hitting power and speed depend on three factors

A. The driving force, that is to say, force produced by muscles generating the movement, i.e. agonists, which are the elbow extensors in this case. The greater the driving force, the stronger and quick the blow.

B. Antagonist muscle tension, whose force is opposed to the movement (they perform the opposite movement); flexors (biceps, etc) in this case. The greater tension, the less hitting power and speed. Agonists coordination is governed by the nervous system (when agonist is contracted, antagonist is relaxed). The third section, with its extremely slow movements, can help to develop this coordination. It makes you more and more efficient in contracting extensors and relaxing flexors.

C. Elastic resistance of conjunctive tissue: muscles, tendons, etc. should stretch when launching the blow. The lesser the resistance they exert, the more powerful and quick the blow. This tissue are stretched in an active way in the fourth section of the form (in contrast to classic stretching, which is passive). To achieve this, certain mental image is used which helps lengthening. So, sections 3 and 4 not only cultivate Chi and are beneficial for your health, but hey also improve your hitting effectiveness.

3. Internal organs are stimulated through a different exercise of section 4, where lungs are emptied at maximum while performing certain movements with breathing making a high-pitched lengthy sound. Abdomen is contracted, bringing your belly button closer to your spine forming a great cavity, just like in the Yoga exercise called "Uddiyana Bandha". This exercise intensively works obliques and transverse muscles of visceral ptosis (drooping organs like stomach). It also stimulates internal organs functions and abdominal nervous plixes and is beneficial for constipation.

4. Perineum muscles (anus and surrounding areas) are stimulated in the adduction position, thus helping to prevent anus prolapses.

Psychological aspects
Deep abdominal breathing, focusing on belly and leg position, creates a mental relaxation state which in physiology is known as "cerebral cortex protective inhibition". It tends to empty your mind from thoughts, thus providing cerebral cortex a rest similar to deep sleep. This is another meaning of "Siu Nim Tao", "little idea", i.e., to thing less and less. Here we find a link to Buddhist meditation (Chan, Zen, in Japanese), in which you maintain a state of inner peace nothing can alter, while keeping full lucidity to (not half slept). This condition of interior silence is ideal under any circumstances, especially in a fight, as senses and reflexes display maximum reaction capacity.

Training the ancient Siu Nim Tao
serious Wing Tsun fighters must do it every day and spend at least half an hour in doing it.

The chosen place for this should be clean and have fresh air, so it is an ideal exercise to be performed outdoors, if possible (thanks to the intense heat it produces, it can be performed even when it is very cold in winter).

Stomach should be empty for abdominal movements, but no hunger should be felt.

Focus must be maintained in the exercise points, (stance, movements, breathing), not paying attention to anything else. Progression is gradual.

The first hindrance is stance. It must be maintained as much time as possible and gradually increase this time a few minutes every week or 15 days, until 45 minutes are reached in a few months time. Once you are comfortable in this stance, attention can be easily paid to breathing, to make it more and more deep and slow, as well as to movements.

198 The Tao of the action

As one advances in the Style, the feeling of Elastic Energy (Ching) developed in Chisao should integrate with the Vital Energy (Chi) feeling. The Meditation (Chan) and physical/external work should approach. This way, Siu Nim Tao becomes a valuable tool for physical, energy, martial and spiritual development

Sifu Víctor Gutiérrez *199*

CHAPTER IV
Bruce Lee

Global interest for WT started when it became public that Bruce Lee had been a student of Great Master Yip Man in Hong Kong, with whom he had studied WT. Then, WT instructors demand skyrocketed in Europe and America. If WT is probably nowadays the most popular Kung Fu style in the world (after Tai Chi possibly) is mostly due to Bruce Lee. It is somewhat curious that before G. M. Yip Man started his classes in Hong Kong, WT was possibly the most secret style in the world.

As to myself, I was also a Bruce Lee fan in my youth. I practiced Taekwondo and Boxing but, when I knew Bruce Lee had been a WT student I decided to emulated my idol and started training with Sifu K. R. Kernspecht, direct student of G. M. Leung Ting. Some of you may find the following somewhat uncomfortable. To me, as a young Bruce Lee admirer it was hard to accept something which was otherwise obvious. I even hated my masters for "humanizing" Bruce Lee myth. First, I have to state my information sources. Many years ago, my Sifu researched the features of "Bruce Lee-modified Wing Chun". To do so, he traveled to United States and studied with Jesse Glover, the first and, according to many people, the most combative Bruce Lee student. There he trained Chi Sao in a stance where the bodyweight was on the front leg, Bruce Lee-style; Bruce's grappling systems, his strategies, etc. At that time, my Sifu was a power lifter, a big, strong, fast and aggressive man. Lee's system appeared to work really well for him. Some time later, he met G. M. Leung Ting again and, not without certain proud, he told him what he learned in the States. G. M. Leung Ting painfully showed him all gaps and mistakes of grappling, Chi Sao and other techniques my Sifu had taken with him from the US. My Sifu confirmed he had a lot to learn and that making Bruce Lee's techniques on stiff styles fighters is different from applying it against a real WT master like Sigung Leung Ting. In all cases, the result was being hit all around.

My Sifu invited Jesse Glover in two occasions to give seminars in Germany. I personally attended to those seminars so I can talk first-hand. By the way, Glover's style is virtually the same as the so-called "Original Bruce Lee's Jeet Kune Do". His Chi Sao, grappling and penetrations are similar.

I must state that Bruce Lee was a genius, but for reasons different from the generally attributed to him. Bruce Lee arrived to United States just before his eighteenth birthday in order to hold the American citizenship. By chance, he was born in the US so, according to the applicable law, he could get citizenship if claimed it before 18.

18 years are not many years in the subject we are dealing with here, even more when Bruce Lee had only practiced WT for 3 years in Hong Kong. In WT, 3 years is nothing. You can get to know the forms and part of the theory, but 100% application requires much more time. Apart from that, Bruce Lee practiced boxing and, in a superficial way, other Kung Fu styles since he was 13 or 14.

Traditional learning methods were not as open and clear as they are nowadays. G. M. Yip Man was not prone to correct the students and to give explanations, so progress was slower. The master had to know the personality of the student before teaching him the style; he could be betrayed. Additionally to training with G. M. Yip Man, Bruce Lee supplemented his skills attending parallel classes by one of Yip Man's oldest students: Wong Shun Leung.

Objectively, it can be said that the boy who arrived to United States could not be a master in any martial art. In fact, we must wonder: What did Bruce Lee really knew about WT when he got to the States? And how much he did not know?

We can infer this by looking at the amendments he introduced.

The first thing Bruce Lee saw was that the strategy of advancing towards the enemy with a burst of vertical straight punches (see pictures) worked really well. Traditional blocking systems were useless against such an avalanche. This way, he won all fights (see pictures). But Bruce Lee did not know the universal solution yet, as he had not been taught the steps and Chi Gerk techniques (Chi Gerk was the last section of WT empty-hand system). So, he did not know how to defend kicks using his legs and he did it with his hands. Lee's advance mode with a punch burst left all the genital area, belly and legs uncovered, vulnerable to kicks. His solution: advancing faster than the enemy (see pictures). From this point on, speed became a key point in Bruce Lee's system, while in WT it is secondary.

The second thing Bruce Lee discovered was that, if he performed Chi Sao exercises in the adduction front position stance, typical in WT, with people stronger and bigger than him, he fell back. The cause was that Bruce Lee DID NOT KNOW how to absorb and straight force to the ground. Training in this stance is aimed to FORCE YOU to learn how to absorb forces. Not having a master to help him, Bruce Lee could not devise a solution to this problem. As Lee had broken the rule forbidding WT to be taught to non-Chinese people, accepting Western students, he lost any chance to keep on learning WT; he was out of Yip Man's WT family. Bruce Lee was a genius because, although he was a kid, he found new ways and paths in a self-taught way in order to keep on improving. From 18 years-old until his death at 32, Bruce Lee had no master and, although he knew other fighters, it can be stated that he had to create, with very short previous experience, a whole new system. And he succeeded.

This proves that he was a genius. What would have you done in his circumstances? Probably nothing but repeating and repeating what you already knew and keep on hitting the same walls.

Back to the Chi Sao stance, Bruce Lee had to make up for his technical deficiencies adopting a forward weight stance in which force could be easily transferred to the arms.

In the third place, Bruce Lee used blockings (see pictures) for defense, something which does not exist in WT. He used hard blockings because he did not master the for basic cession reactions. Like many other WT men who confined themselves to practicing Chi Sao at low to medium speed, he could not adapt and give way to boxing hits. So, he had to discard the four reactions (Bong, Tan, Cham and Kao Sao). Additionally, he could not use the Moving Turn to get out of the attack line giving way to the force anymore, as he changed the base stance for a weight-forward stance (which stance is, by the way, similar to Philippine Escrima's). So, he found a new defensive arsenal in Boxing and other disciplines. He started to use boxing-like dodging and blocking. To improve his attacks he undertook an exhaustive research of feints used in Boxing.

What did Bruce Lee know about Chi Sao? Apparently, not much:
- One-hand Chi Sao.
- Poon Sao (rolling).
- Some elementary locks.
- Some come-ins.

Bruce Lee could not apply Chi Sao with the variations he introduced, but he managed to adapt the locks. In fact, locks became his "hallmark", greatly confusing other styles fighters.

Many people now believe that locks are the main WT technique, which could not be further from the truth. When you lock your opponent's arm, your own arm is locked too! In WT you always stick to your opponent until a gap is created. There are a lot of ways for avoiding locks (see pictures). Locks are really effective when you catch your opponent's both arms using just one of yours, and you leave no room for him to release while you hit him using your free hand (see pictures).

On the other hand, Bruce Lee had no Master to guide him, as explained above, so he could not notice the little mistakes in his locks. This "little mistakes" were openings, gaps through which the opponent could hit him and avoid the lock (see pictures). Even my own Sifu K. R. Kernspecht did not notice those faults until he crossed arms with his Sifu, G. M. Leung Ting. A certain degree of sensitiveness and technique is required to be able to take advantage of those gaps.

All in all, Bruce Lee gradually moved to a system based on visual perception and speed. He had to develop an extraordinary sense of distance and great mobility in order to get in and out quickly. Conversely, WT is based in advancing while cutting off your opponent's movements and applying sensitiveness staying stuck to him. In comparative terms, Bruce Lee's system requires more youth and athletic skills, and it leaves some factors to fate when paying so much attention to visual perception and distance assessment.

Regarding hitting power, he also had to find alternatives here. Bruce Lee still ignored how to create explosive power with shoulders parallel in frontal stance. He simply lacked training time with a master. But his genius did not stop there. He researched and got to find out other way of gaining hitting power: using the coordinated turn of shoulders and trunk combined with legs momentum and weight change. So, Bruce Lee did not launch the one-inch-punch in frontal stance, but turning his shoulders. He added Boxing punches to the straight punch burst, as boxing blows work better in the weight-forwards stance. He also introduced Finger Jabs combining them with locks. He took kicks from other styles, required for his displacement system to work out.

Bruce Lee never arrived to know the advanced step system of WT. So, he devised his own system, quite similar in mechanics principles to Philippine Escrima. His moving speed was legendary.

Bruce lee was a genius because he managed to overcome his initial limitations using effort and creativity. And all that in a virtually self-teaching way. But he was not an expert in Wing Chun or any Kung Fu style. Actually, this condition does not tarnish his image at all; it praises it. An inexperienced boy, confronting the world alone, was able to amaze everyone with his genius.

Rest in peace.

詠 春 拳

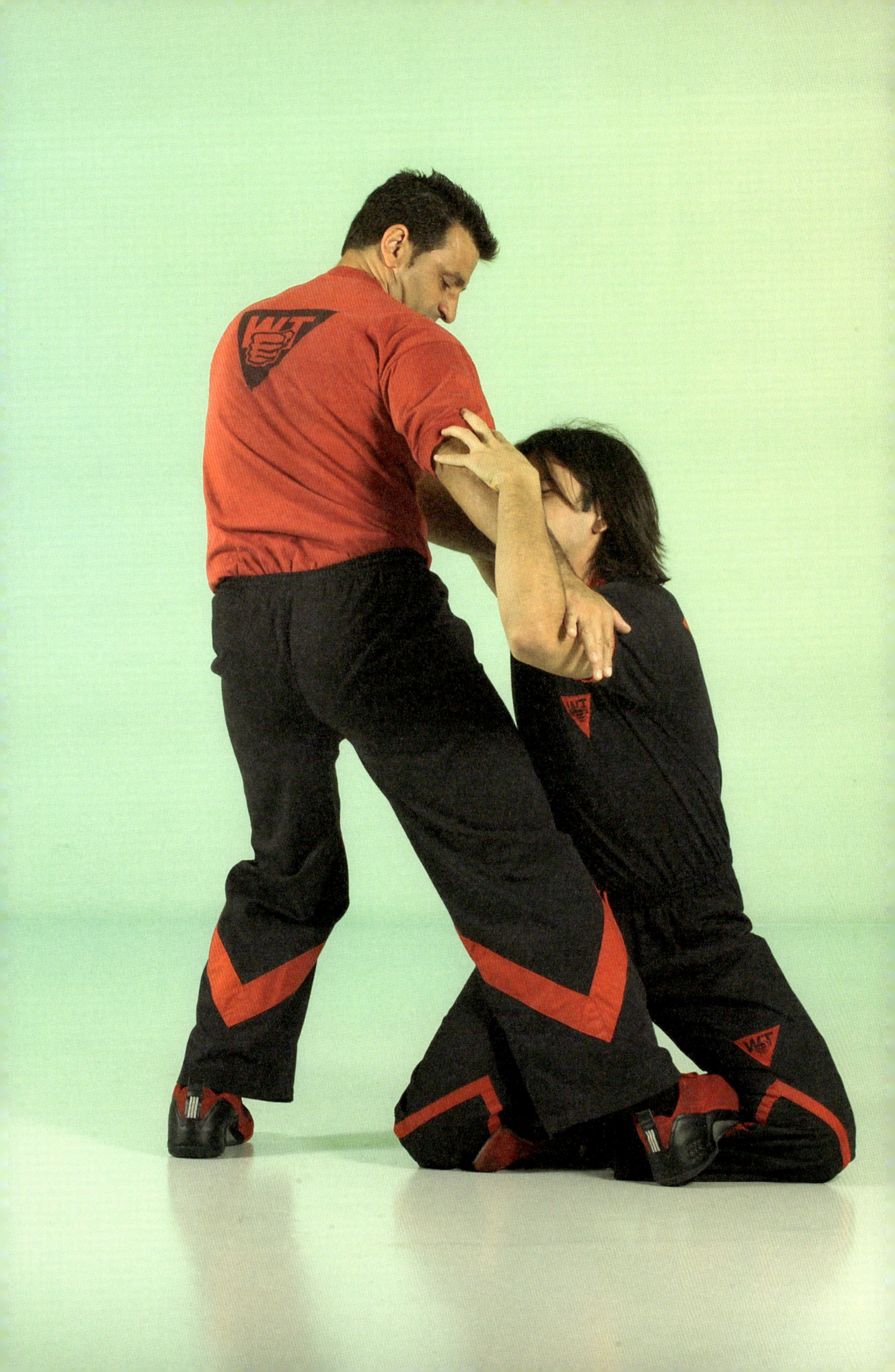

CHAPTER V
WT Today – moving forwards or backwards?

WT System experienced an extraordinary expansion, especially in Europe. Our style possesses very special features making it one of the most attractive martial arts:
- Proven effectiveness.
- No need of great physical qualities.
- Scientific rationality captivating many engineers, physicists, doctors, biologists, etc.
- Softness enabling permanent progress even at advanced years.
- Complexity keeping interest over decades, as there are always new things to lean.
- No injuries related to exhaustion or movement, thanks to a proprietary kinesiology not producing joint injuries.
- Well-structured organization.

However, WT also present some "little faults or hindrances"
- As a system based on developing inner "sensitiveness", it cannot be learned visually. Frequent contact with an instructor and training with partners are a must. In other words, you cannot make great progress in WT training alone. And you will not learn anything just "watching".
- Also, a great deal of responsibility, attention and "talent" is required for the part of the student if he/she wants to understand the principles underlying the exercises performed in class and benefit from them. A certain intellectual ability for research and analysis is important to progress in WT.

So, the following statement can be understood: "WT takes the risk of dying by success". Why? Wherever WT is popular a great boom occurred. As a consequence, the number of students in each class skyrocketed. The first consequence of crowding is the lower time the instructor can personally devote to each student. The second consequence is derived from the first -- as "feeling" cannot be transferred trough correction and guidelines from Sifu when crossing hands with him, skills level decreased.

Also, many students lack the toughness, discipline and interest to take the pains of doing their best and correct each other during the whole class so quality level drops.

However, not only the students or the lack of time can be exclusively blamed. Many instructors are starting to show some idleness or indulgence; they take the easy way. So, many of them do not freely train with their students anymore, making them attack the way they want. Instead of that, they confine themselves to practice Chi Sao or Lat Sao according to the programs, losing adaptability and combat spirit. If Chi Sao and Lat Sao are not freely practiced with any kind of people, the own heart of WT is betrayed.

In seminars given by Great Masters such as Sigung Leung Ting or Dai Sifu Kernspecht, where students and instructors are put together, I often observed something funny.

Instead of take the chance to train with their partners, instructors in the same or higher level, in order to progress, many teachers avoid to do their best for fear of being defeated by other partner and looking "ridiculous" in front of their students. So, a companionship climate has established in seminars. As an unwritten law, nobody really attacks.

Outcome: Nowadays, many instructors are unable to succeed in free combat against a well trained person.

Are there any solutions? Yes

One of them is to increase the degree of supervision over instructors, re-testing them regularly and stripping them of grades if they do not match up. Other option is to give instructor-only seminars, with no risk of a student watching his instructor being defeated. Finally, to control overcrowding in classes and to instill a sense of mutual cooperation among students to remove competitiveness and make them help each other to rectify and progress.

APPENDIX
The advanced level

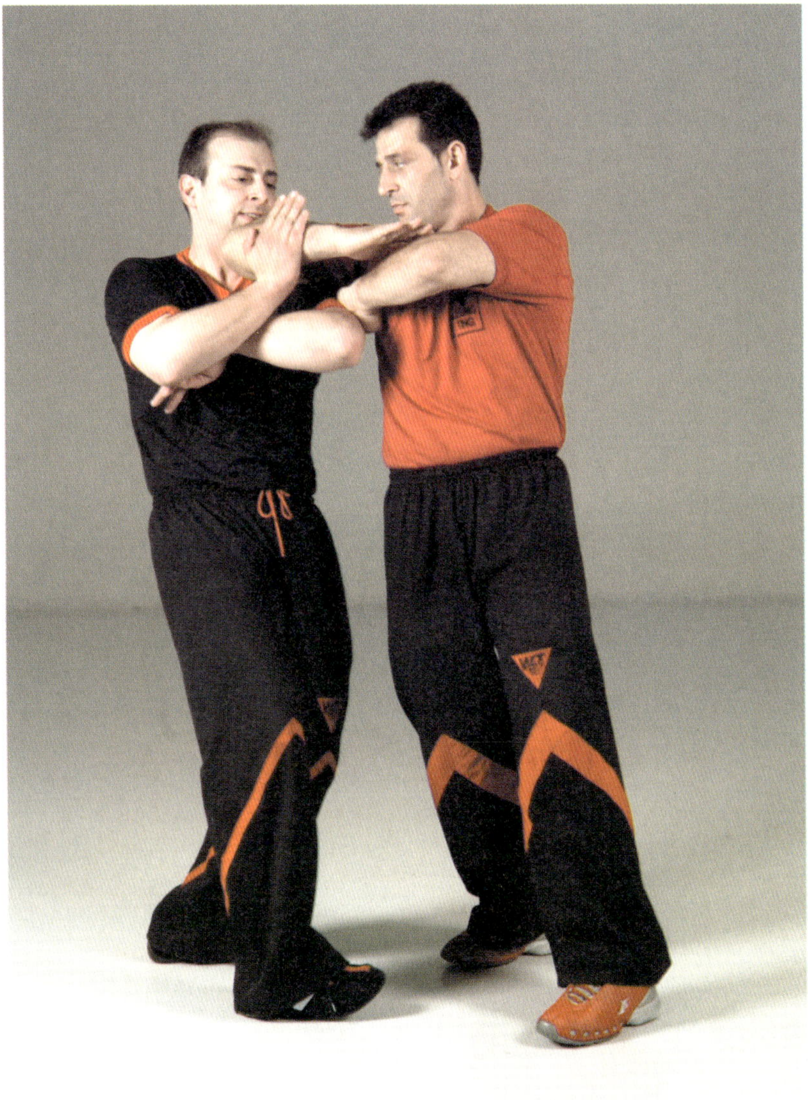

WT, Advanced combat techniques

Technical progression in WT can be divided into three levels
- Basic or beginner.
- Intermediate.
- Advanced.

There are major differences between these levels, especially between the advanced level and the previous two, where the difference is so huge that they almost can be considered as different martial arts. In fact, this would be the conclusion of a layman watching the front and vertical stance and the straight punches performed in basic and intermediate levels comparing them with the continuous turns, flexions and extensions of the trunk, linked to light steps and straight and round open-hand blows performed in advanced level.

A full description of all three levels and their techniques in our system are described below:

BEGINNER
Grades: The twelve student grades.
Techniques: Universal Solution, Kicks + Chain Punches + Steps.
- Self-defense: any distance, individual opponent, multiple opponents, defense against weapons.
- Forms: SNT, CKT.
- Chi-Sao: Darn-Chi-Sao (one arm).
- Poon-Sao: rolling and attacking every gap (both arms).
- First Chi-Sao section: includes, Lap-Sao, bridge crossing, turns, attacks, holds, etc.
- Lat-Sao.

Psychomotor coordination: arm-scapular waist-hips-legs connection is developed in a basic fashion, i.e. with just a few joint-springs -- the spine acts as a block stiffly connecting scapular waist, pelvis and hips.

Force coming from the opponent is mainly absorbed in the scapular waist thanks to the "spring" in the shoulder blade.

INTERMEDIATE
Grades: First and second technician grades.
Techniques: Chi-Sao sections corresponding to each grade.
Lat-Sao applications.

Psychomotor coordination: scapular waist and pelvis are connected through the spine in a more complex fashion, using the raquis as a spring with multiple stations. This way, the opponent's force is much better absorbed, with less movement, and headed to the ground. The fighter is much more connected to the ground, his stability is multiplied. You learn to draw force for your blows from your lower belly (lower Dantien), so you can hit relaxed but very powerfully, although you feel like not using almost no strength. The Dantien or pelvic region starts to be the source of all your power and ability to absorb your opponents' energy. This training is very important, and a necessary condition to get to learn the advanced level techniques.

Stance is frontal, but short-length flexion movements are performed.

ADVANCED LEVEL
It is divided into empty-hand work and weapons work.

Grades: third and fourth technician grades, fifth practical grade (empty-hand); sixth, seventh and eighth practical graces (weapons) for long pole and butterfly knives.

Empty-hand techniques:
- **Forms:** Biu-Tzi (flying fingers).
- **Wooden dummy** - 116 movements.
- **Chi-Sao:** relevant sections.
- **Chi-Gerk** (sticky legs).
- **Lat-Sao applications.**

Weapon techniques:
Pole form and exercises.
- Sticky pole. Combat.
- Knife form and applications.

Which are the indicators of a student's level?

Traditionally, forms were used to establish the level of a WT student. For instance, someone knowing the third form should be in the advanced level, even more if he mastered the wooden dummy form. It is said that Great Master Yip Man only taught the whole dummy form to five people. When Leung Bik, son of Leung Jan, met a teenager Yip Man, the first thing he asked him was if he knew the Chun-Kiu form, in order to ascertain his level.

However, forms are not the key element which make the student's skills grow. The exercises associated to these forms (steps, punches, kicks, Chi-Sao, Lat-Sao) are what make you progress. Any person can learn all the WT forms, including the wooden dummy form, in just a few months; but his fighting skills and understanding of WT would hardly advance.

I have had students who knew all the forms of our style, even the pole and knives forms, and had been issued certificates acknowledging them as experts in the "whole style". However, their actual level was second student grade. They could not apply any of the techniques in the forms, as combat skills are not trained in forms, not even in "pure" technique. Forms and Chi-Sao are not enough either, you need Lat-Sao to be able to apply the movements in combat.

The WT learning method is: First learn the "correct form", relating to angles and proper stance both in individual movements (Forms, Taos) and in Chi-Sao exercises, being the latter the most relevant. Through the training of the correct form (stance), the correct sensation is knowable. Once you master sensation, form (stance) is forgotten.

This means that, through Chi-Sao you learn the right psychomotor coordination to connect all body part and "springs" in a global harmonic action. This "connected body" is perceived as a group of technical, subjective techniques which are very precise and definite. These sensations are refined and evolved when progressing in the style. When a high psycho-somatic integration level is achieved, it can be said that the sensation is mastered. Then you can start breaking the much-trumpeted "correct stances" and achieve the same efficiency by keeping your body fully connected; this is the advanced level.

WT Taos (SIU-NIN-TAO, CHUM-KIU-TAO, BIU-TZI-TAO) are not choreographies representing combat situations. Their objective is so different:

1. They educate the right stances in relaxation, i.e. psychomotor coordination, etc. They strengthen and give flexibility to muscles, tendons, etc. In sum, they improve health.

2. They involve, like a dictionary or encyclopedia, ideas, tactics and technical principles, both martial and health-related (which nowadays is known as Qi Gong or Chi-Kung). A gesture or movement can imply different concepts which should be developed in the form of Chi-Sao,

Lat-Sao or therapeutic exercises. If the hidden meaning of a movement is unknown, the key book embodied by the form cannot be used.

However what makes you acquire the skills and sensations of a "connected body" are not the forms but the Chi-Sao exercises. Once these sensations are assimilated through Chi-Sao, they are translated to individual exercises of the forms by way of memory and imagination, similarly to Schultz's autogenous training. So, the paradox is served -- the forms contain the concepts giving birth to Chi-Sao and Lat-Sao tactics, but Chi-Sao and Lat-Sao training offer the sensations required to really develop the forms, making them "internal" exercises. Recently, this has been called martial QI GONG (CHI-KUNG) or INNER KUNG FU.

That is the reason why so many differences in SNT or CKT can be observed if performed by a basic or intermediate level student or by an expert. Externally they look the same movements, but internally they are completely different.

Features of empty-hand advanced level. Offensive aspects:
- Hitting power.
- Third form - Biu-Tzi-Tao.

Starting from the ability to use arm-scapula-spine-pelvis (dantien) connections, you evolve improving the dynamics of strong hitting with short movements, already pre-developed in intermediate level. In advance level, front stance is broken, your body turns at the same time you move your bodyweight and the spine is flexed or extended. This way, hitting power is multiplied. Also, attacking, surfaces and angles change. Now, open-hand becomes an essential weapon -- fingers, palms, hand-edges and forearms. Although the name of the third form (Biu-Tzi) is often translated as "flaying/penetrating fingers", fingers are not mainly used actually but the hand edges and palms. Blows are straight or round, top-down or bottom-up. They are not like Shuto blows in Karate but a sort of clap with the longest and most external edge headed to the neck, jaw, throat or face. The power released hitting with a "connected body" is enormous, getting even to break the neck.

Other punch in the third form is the hook. Some people think that WingTsun only uses straight punches. Obviously, they ignore the second form, Chum-Kiu, in which a bottom-up round punch, similar to boxing uppercut, can be found; and the third, Biu-Tzi, where we find the hook **(picture 222)**.

This hook is used in short distance, using the bodyweight fall, turn and "full-body connection" to create a fabulous impact. The hook is used after having induced the gap to "cross the bridge", never in longer distance. Top-down elbows are very characteristic of this level. They have both offensive and defensive features, as explained below. These elbows are not aimed only to hit your opponent but also to open his guard to get in with bursts of hand-edge blows headed to neck and jaw. Like in any top-down hit, bodyweight, turn and "connected body" are used to create devastating power.

Techniques transmitted in Biu-Tzi are mainly offensive. Your attack penetrates your opponent's guard and protects you at the same time, using bursts of hand-edge/palm blows covering any kind of straight or round counterattacks. The objective is to get very close and completely neutralize your opponent while being able to hit him continuously. After every hit, one hand goes back to protect both central and peripheral lines in a round movement. At the same time, the other hand hits at full power. This burst is quite different from the straight punches one. It is also possible to develop variations of the universal solutions in difficult situations:

- In a totally open guard: arms outstretched, etc. **(pictures 223 to 226.)**

216 *The Tao of the action*

223

224

225

226

- If attacked from one side, (picture 227).

Regarding leg techniques, in Biu-Tzi only a sweeping can be found, which introduces future Chi-Gerk (sticky legs) training which is performed after studying the wooden dummy form.

This sweeping is applied combined with a Biu-Tzi-specific double hold which presses certain sensitive points in the forearm. The final result is a tremendous throw, learnt in the wooden dummy form, **(picture 228.)**

Defensive aspects of the third form

The four basic reactions (Bong, Tan, Chum and Kau-Sao) are shortened to the point they can hardly be recognized. Bong-Sao becomes a sort of defensive/offensive elbow hit which gives way to pressure coming from outside to inside to get in at the same time with an elbow blow or Fak-Sao (edge-blow) **(picture 230).** Similarly, Tan-Sao becomes almost imperceptible, as it turns into a palm or edge blow immediately. Chum-Sao is now a simple almost lazy gesture which, using the "human spring" trained in this advanced level, lets your opponent hit enter until your ear, neutralized with perfect control, creating an insuperable opening through which you can hit as much as you want **(picture 229).**

220 The Tao of the action

In Biu-Tzi we find an apparently anodyne and ineffective movement: deeply bending your body and passing your hands between your legs and then rising and bending back your body. This movement has health-related benefits, but also martial applications. The spine movement has to be combined with the aforementioned techniques. The resulting image can apparently be similar to Jackie Chan's "drunken monkey" style and it is used in a extremely short distance **(pictures 231, 234).**

Wooden dummy form

The next step is the wooden dummy form and its Chi-Sao and Chi-Gerk sections and its Lat-Sao applications. With this training, connections are improved; they go down to your legs to be used to kick, sweep, destroy members (ankles, knees, hips) dislocate with your legs and improve displacements. Now you give way and move forwards at the same time while hitting and using your steps to reach your opponent's back (Picture 235).

Chi-Gerk is the culmination of empty-hand techniques and provides terrible skills for absorbing and neutralizing sweepings, low kicks, knee blows and take-downs. As a result, your WT becomes a style in which leg techniques are essential. A WT expert mastering the advanced level, when contacting his/her opponent, feels how the attack's kinetics passes through his/her body to the ground thanks to the internal connections created by training and, like a spring, he/she releases the accrued energy in a blow.

It is often heard about "chi hits" in which "no muscle force "but "internal energy" is used. How can this be construed? If this would be an objective fact, this would mean levitation, as to stand-up you need to contract your leg muscles; then it would be absurd and easily refutable. Outside WT, great masters of internal styles (Xing Yi, Tai Ji, Ba Gua, etc.) undoubtedly state that "internal energy" projection needs muscle contraction. Then, what is the real meaning of those words? From a subjective point of view, this expression is totally admissible, as the feeling of hitting with your "connected body" is exactly this. It seems you do not make any force, but the impact is enormous. This sensation is the "internal force", something personal which cannot be understood by anyone not experiencing it. It is not something like a laser beam, as some people pretend. It is a mental effect which produces an effect in your movements making all muscles in your body unite in a single explosive gesture.

Palm blows in the wooden dummy sides, especially, can be felt in other parts of the body, as the shock wave is propagated until impacting an internal organ (kidney, spleen, liver, etc.)

Once this sensation is perfected, it can be used in styles other than WT to hit powerfully and fluently (Boxing, Tai Chi, Escrima) although their technical structure is different.

Other remarkable aspect of dummy techniques and Chi-Gerk is that they are very useful against take-downs, locks, holds or throws, possibly due to an influence from Chinese wrestling.

In short, when the student gets to the advanced level, he/she is captivated by what seems to be a new martial art, which actually is based on the same principles but presents a vast technical deepness.

235

Index

PROLOGUE 5

1ST PART: WT: TAO IN ACTION 7
    CHAPTER I: MAIN PRINCIPLES WT CHI SAO 9
    CHAPTER II: THE TRAINING METHOD 22
    CHAPTER III: THE YIN-YANG HARMONY
    IN THE PSYCHOLOGICAL FIELD: THE ART OF MEDITATION 32

2ND PART: HOW TO PRACTICE WT CHI SAO 37
    CHAPTER I: CONCEPTS AND STRATEGY 38
    CHAPTER II: ONE TECHNIQUE VS. ONE MILLION 45
    CHAPTER III: HOW TO LEARN 53
    CHAPTER IV: CHI SAO PROGRESSION 61
    CHAPTER V: FUNDAMENTALS AND METHODS OF POWER TRAINING 95

3RD PART: SELF-DEFENSE 118
    CHAPTER I: WT APPLIED TO SELF-DEFENSE 119
    CHAPTER II: SELF-DEFENSE AGAINST MULTIPLE ATTACKS 128
    CHAPTER III: SELF-DEFENSE AGAINST ARMED PEOPLE 133
    CHAPTER IV: THE SECRETS OF COMBAT EFFECTIVENESS 141
    CHAPTER V: ANTI-GRAPPLING 154

4TH PART: WT AND SOCIETY 170
    CHAPTER I: THE NUN NG MUI LEGEND AND AN ANALYSIS
    OF WT'S TECHNICAL FEATURES 171
    CHAPTER II: WOMEN AND MARTIAL ARTS 175
    CHAPTER III: WT, HEALTH AND CHI KUNG 188
    CHAPTER IV: BRUCE LEE 200
    CHAPTER V: WT TODAY - MOVING FORWARDS OR BACKWARDS? 206

APPENDIX: THE ADVANCED LEVEL 208